On Life

Path of a Woman's Soul

Poems by
Carol Melber

Contributing Photographer
Diane Mateer

ISBN:978-0-9983486-2-9
Library of Congress Reg. No. TX 9-004-763

Manufactured in the United States of America

Some photographs are by the Author
contributed from her private collection

Content and Poems

PROLOGUE

Two sisters were born 7 years apart, The first in 1957 and The second in 1964. To their amazement and delight, in 2021 the first turns 64 and the second turns 57. They chose this year to collaborate on a project that showcases their talents, love for each other, and their ever-growing zest for life and all that it entails.

57/64

64/57

DEDICATION

We dedicate this book to everyone who is a sister, has a sister, or knows a sister (sister Nuns count).

Rugged Road

Stay the rugged road, it knows no forward path.

Circles so commonplace yet not anticipated

may be welcome when lessons learned one day are forgotten

or misread by the heart.

Ah, to have some other chance of living to a different ending

than that destined for one who burns bridges.

The one who falls perilously, perhaps to death, a sacrifice to

the passing of an emotional stage.

Stark naked bear the sorry truth of errs.

Humiliation strengthens determination

for one who walks with or follows

in the shadows of all the holy hopefuls

trekking the rugged road.

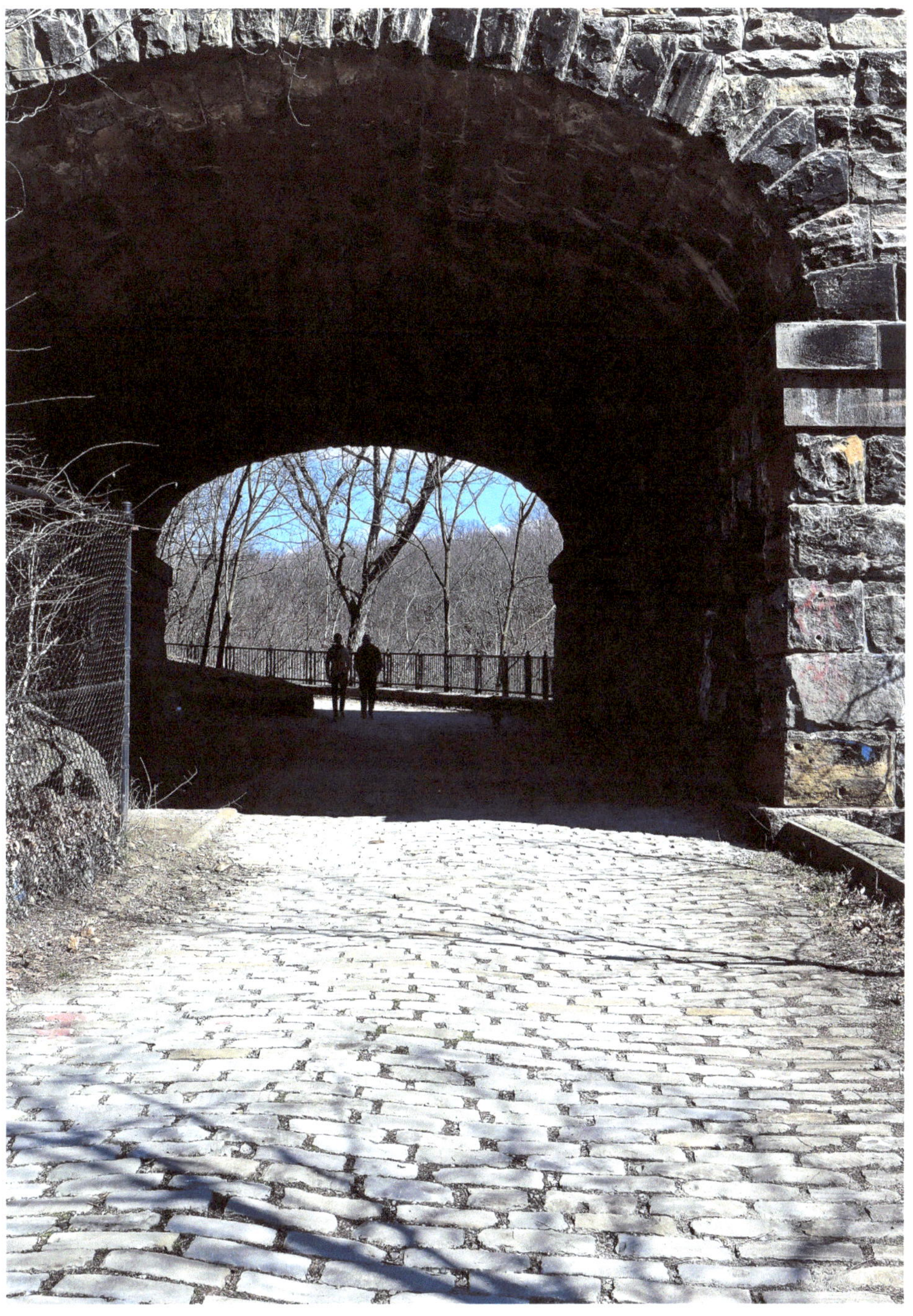

Fantasy

Take me or let me take you on a journey.

We will be plastered in bliss,

orgasmic seeds

captured by the wind of our imagination.

We will be free and fleeing yet

deceptively lingering for a little while,

if only in our minds, returning as we may.

You and me or each alone.

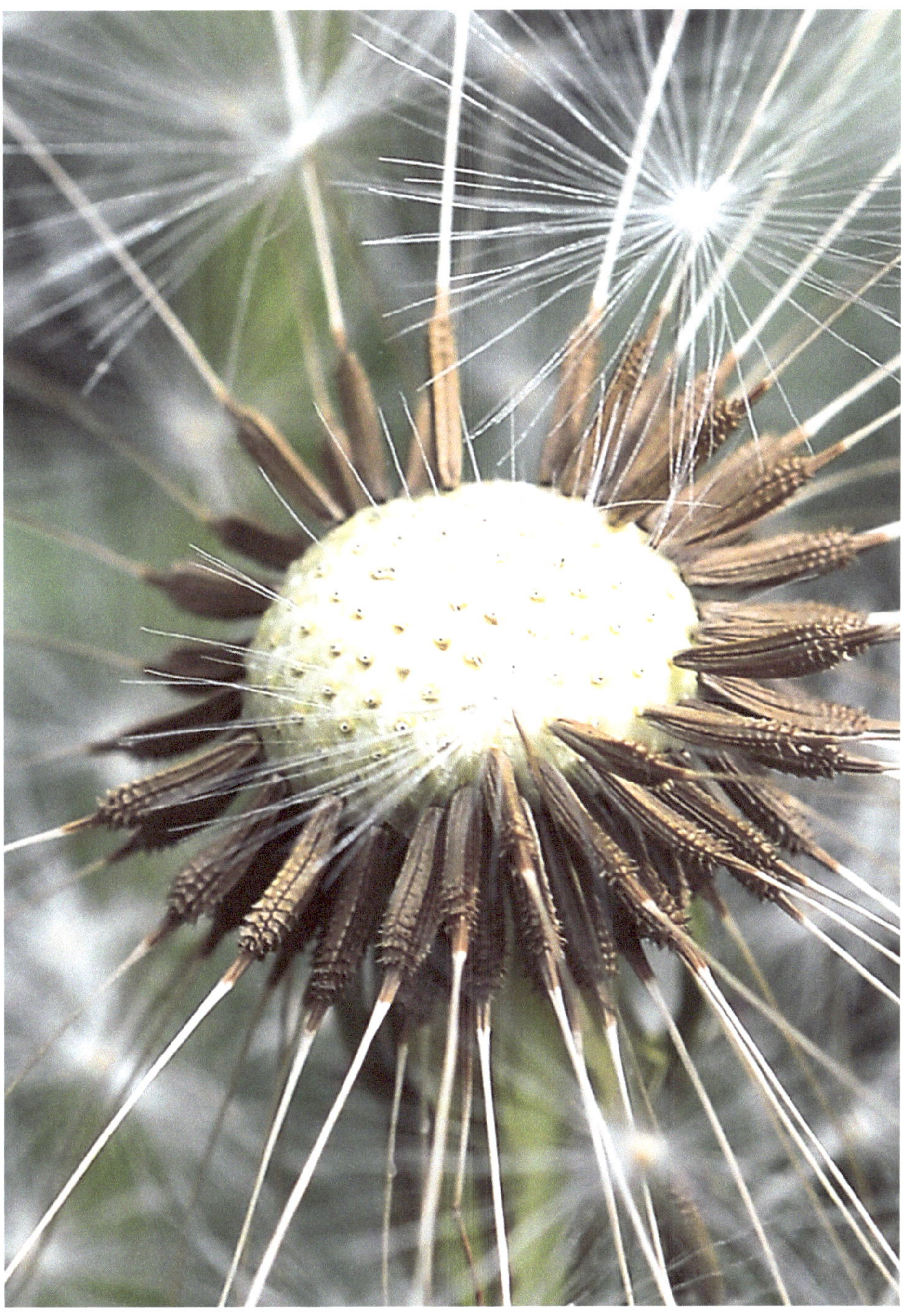

Daydream

Is there ever time enough to waste on thinking of nothing?

How many seconds, to minutes, to hours, to days, to years,

do we squander our time in daydream?

We act as though we have control of the time we have

by controlling the way we spend our time.

So in daydream we choose to pass the time away.

But are we wasting time or

is it sometimes necessary

for the mind to think of nothing?

Are we being lazy, or

are we resetting our brain circuitry

in preparation for the next phase

of our emotional and spiritual development?

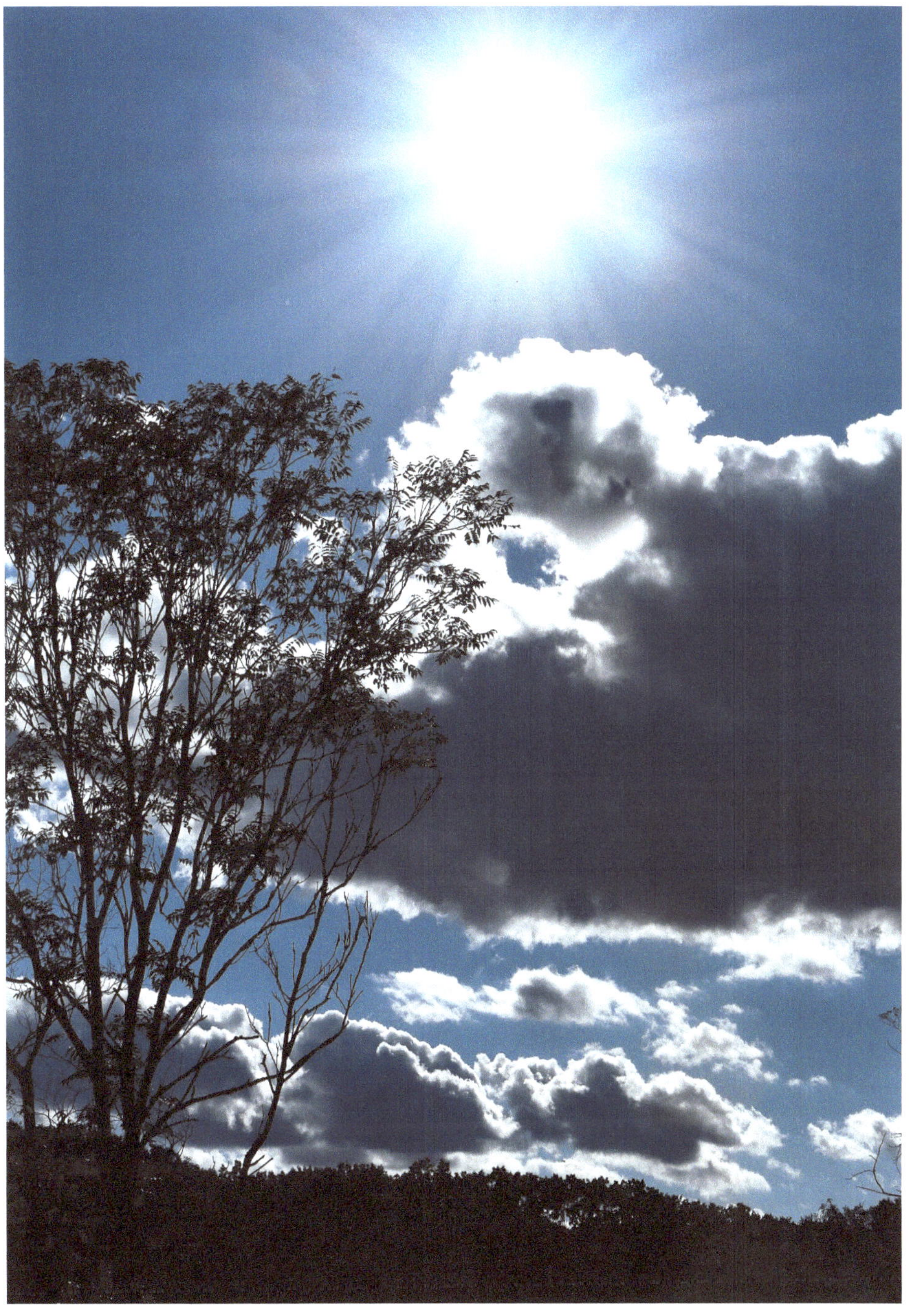

Deception

When she ventured out that night

she was not sure what lay ahead, but she really did not care much.

He must have believed that she did not care for herself at all.

At first he played advisor

and she listened hard for every word.

He carried her politeness in his pocket nestled

between his car keys and small change.

Suspecting nothing, he continued and she did not waiver.

As she stood before him

he spewed one small lie after another.

When he noticed her steadfast expression

hinting at game over, she could see that

his image of her was now shaken

and she watched hard for every change.

She watched as though she was outside,

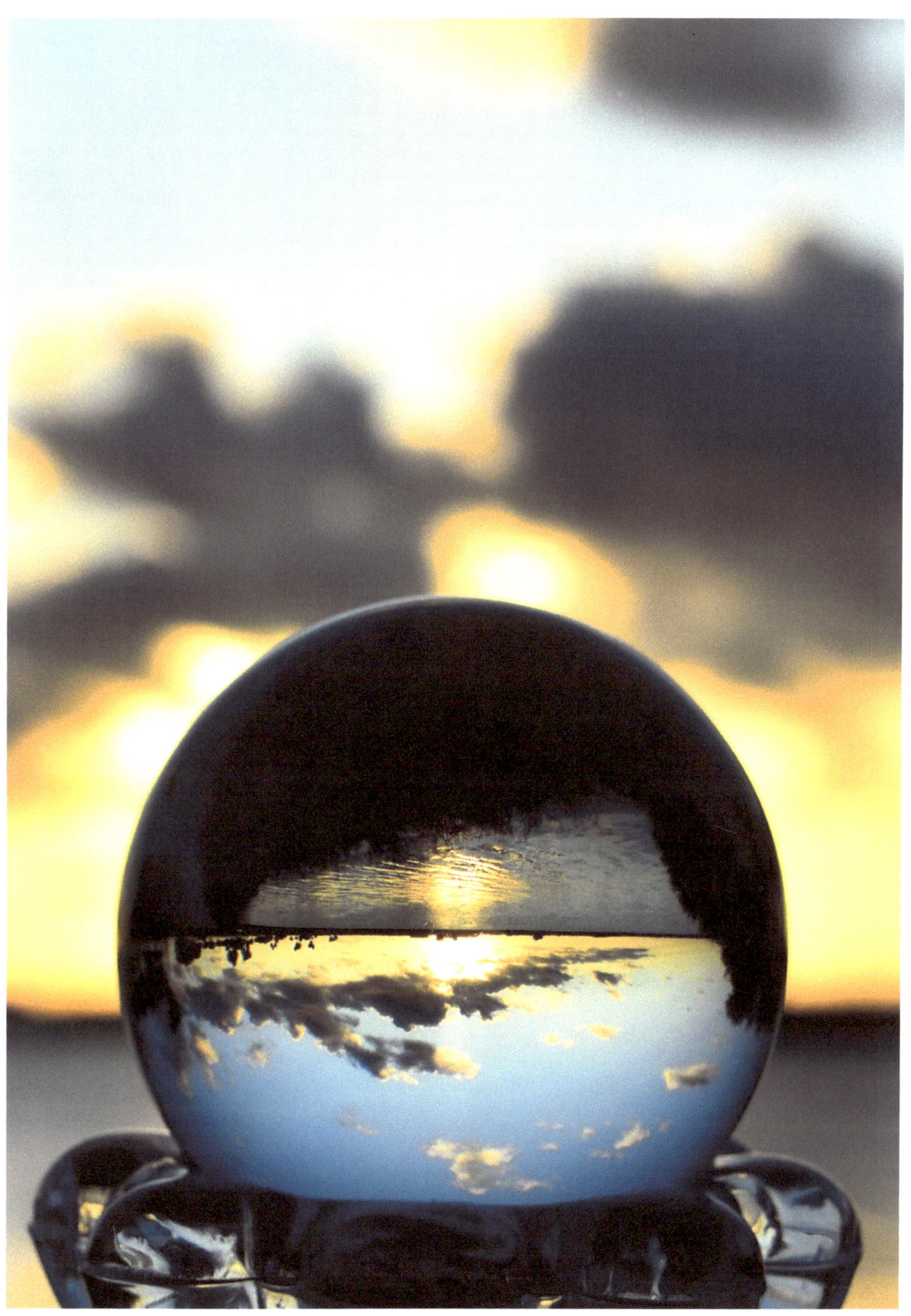

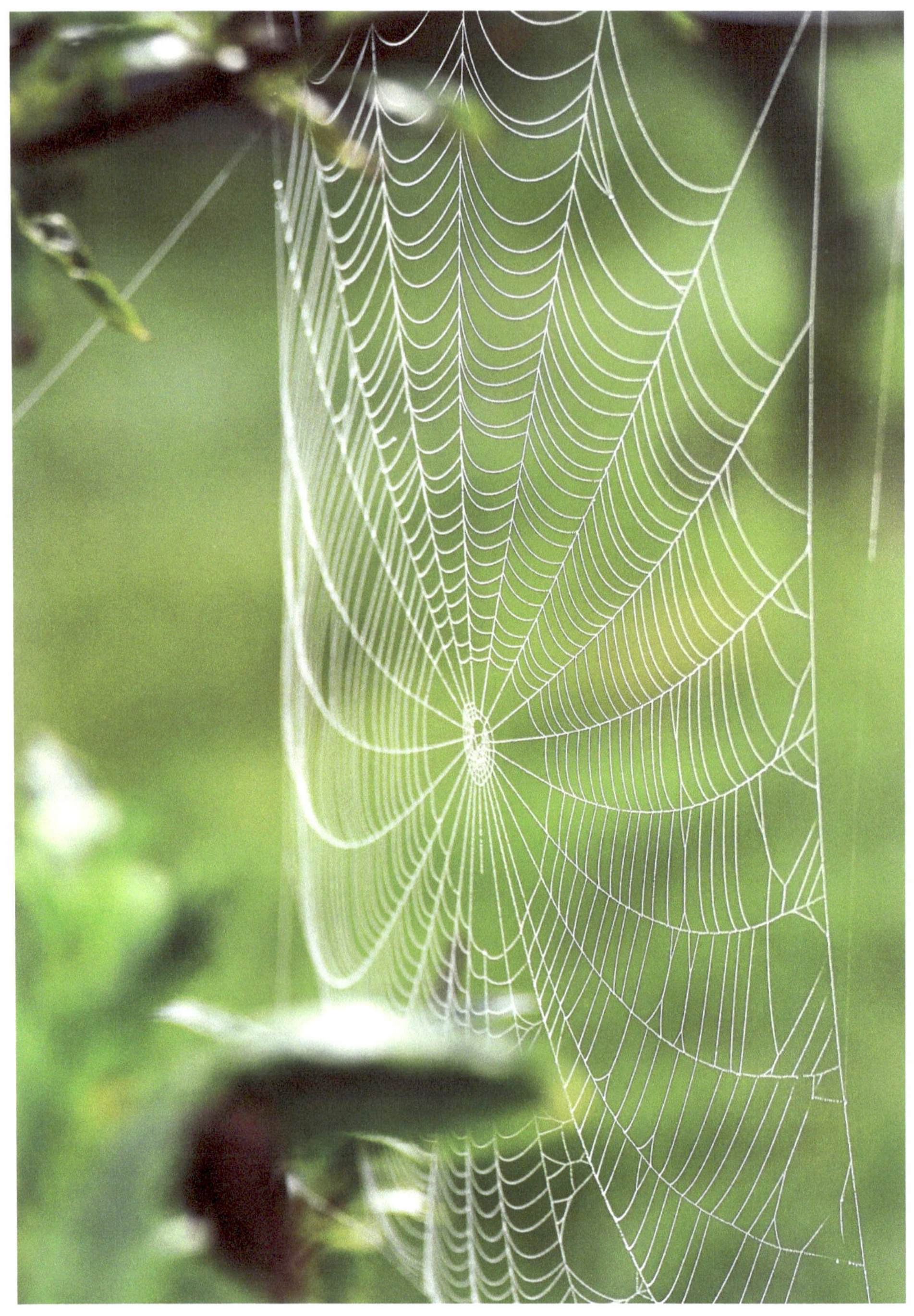

looking in on two other people

engaged in a one-sided conversation.

Like a master he chose his words carefully

and she supposed he fully expected

her to submit to his plan.

He already knew how the night would end-she was predictable.

So he spoke the words that should have set his plan in motion.

But the words triggered deja vu for her

and she saw that he was walking down a stoney path alone.

At that precise moment

she knew that she was ready to make her move in check.

He seemed to believe her excuse but

it did not matter.

She was no longer in the spell

spun by his charming air of sophistication.

She barely noticed his last ditch attempt

to strategize by reminding her of her youth.

She was proud that she had not succumbed

and was ashamed of him for that

without conscience he tried.

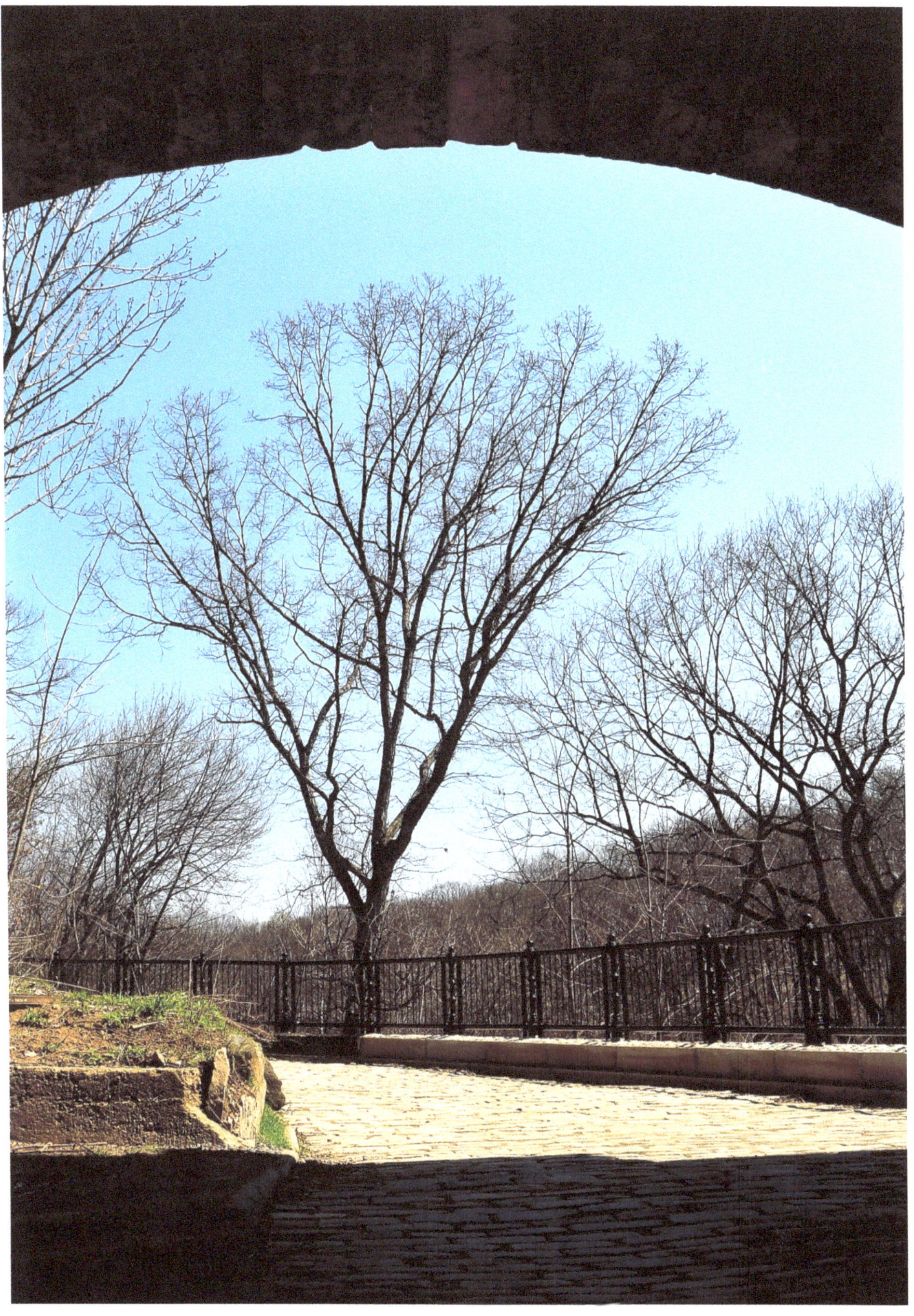

Step by Step

Multiple beginnings and endings.

Streams of enthusiasm, excitement,

and loss.

All along a somewhat reckless path

to complete an education.

Complete only in knowing

that the never-ending yearn for more

will forever render it incomplete.

The same accomplishment

that at first brightens the darkest void

will just as surely bring loneliness as a

mock companion.

This step like all past milestones

is landed heavy, as if to mark

an exclamation point at the finish.

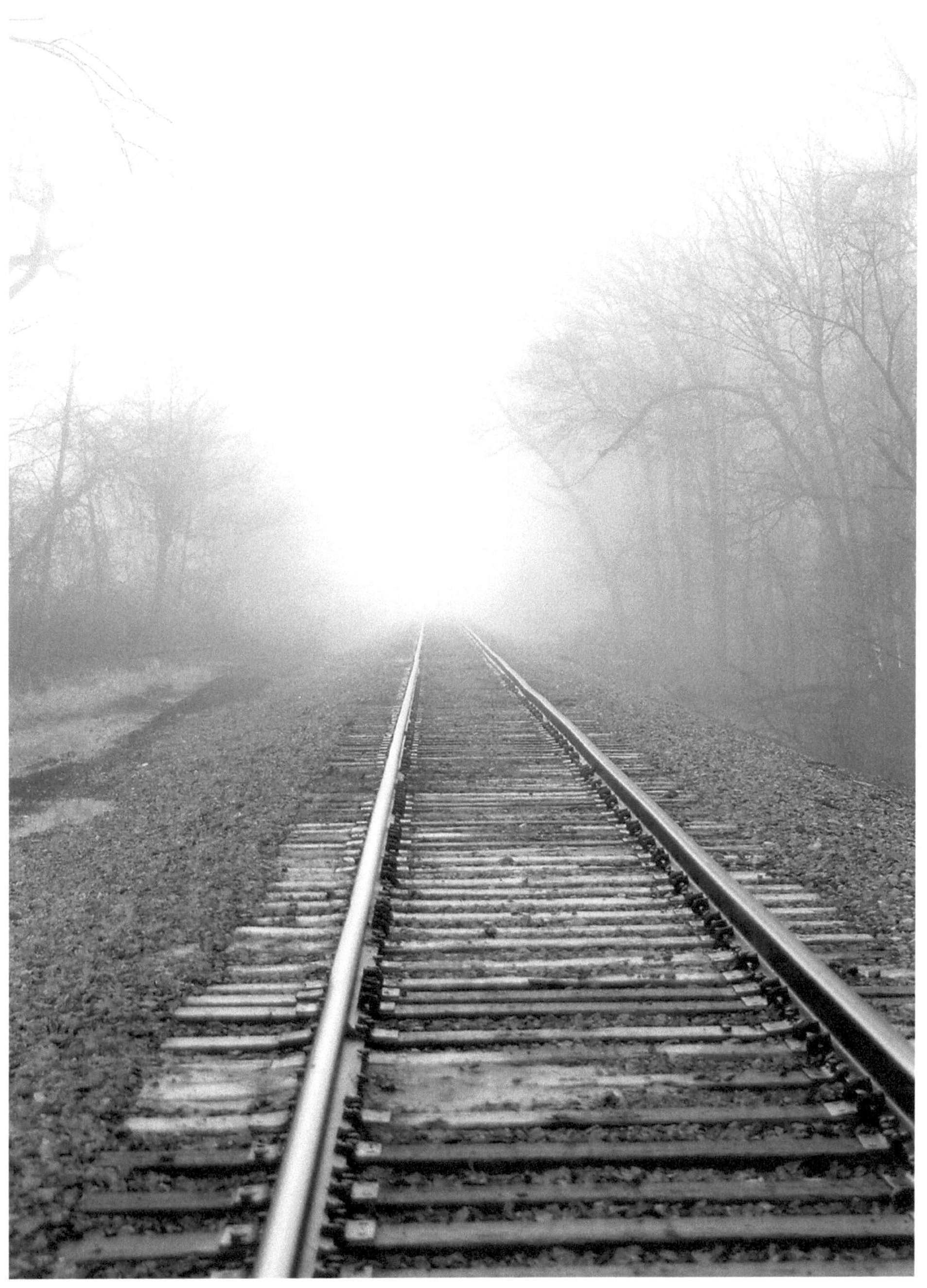

Now the process is done at last.

Yet again, it is not over.

Look there just ahead,

the next step awaits.

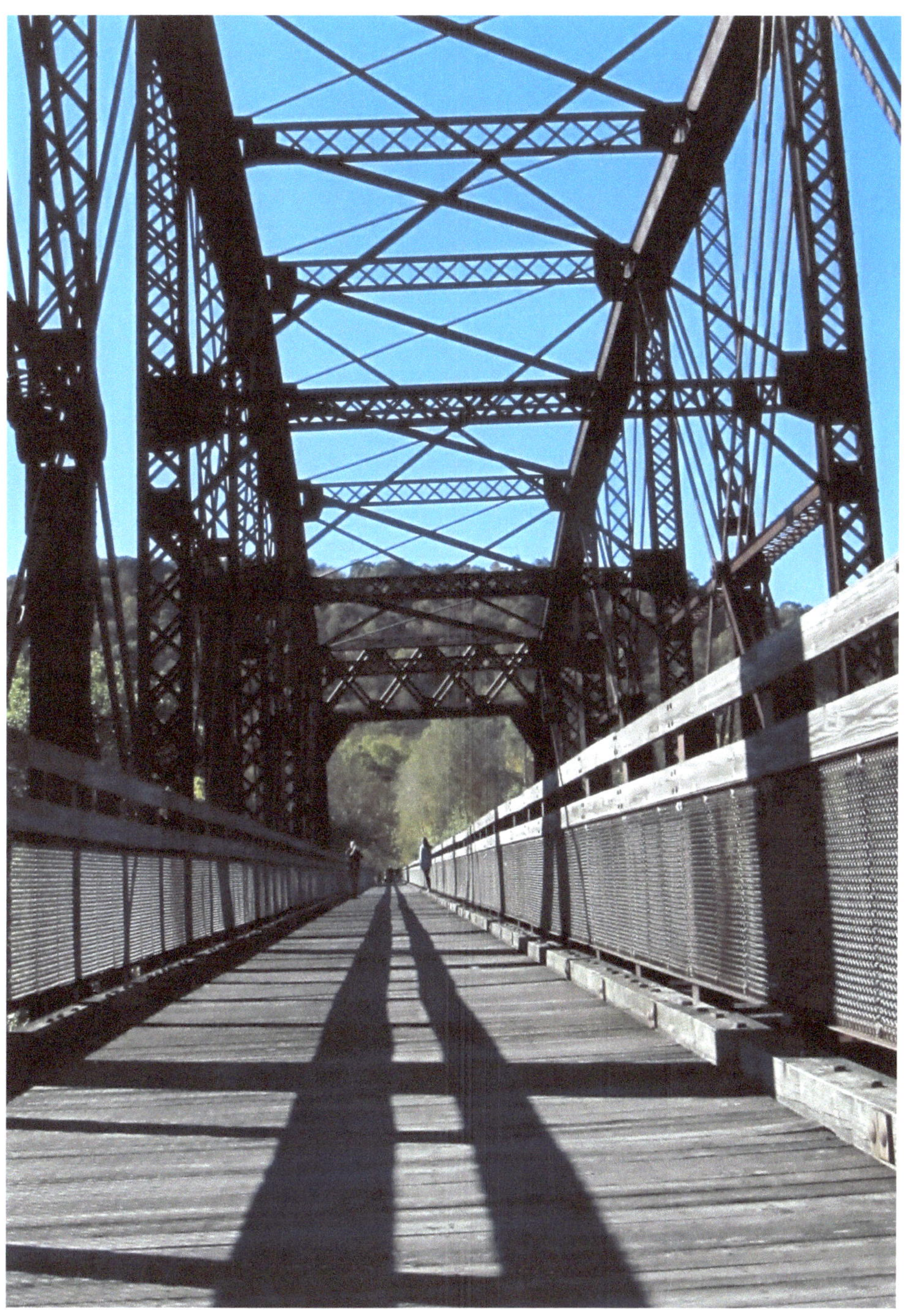

Time

Time moves slowly

for the young and impatient.

The things that matter

are the things yet unexperienced.

The quest to reach the freedom of

independence sometimes outshines the dream

of which to reach requires a discipline.

No matter for the young for whom there is countless time.

The young who dream only of navigating the present time

are thought foolish and yet admired

by the older more burdened by thoughts

of what lies ahead in future time.

For the still climbing younger, the present time can be choking,

suppressive, and unfair.

Future time is coming faster over time

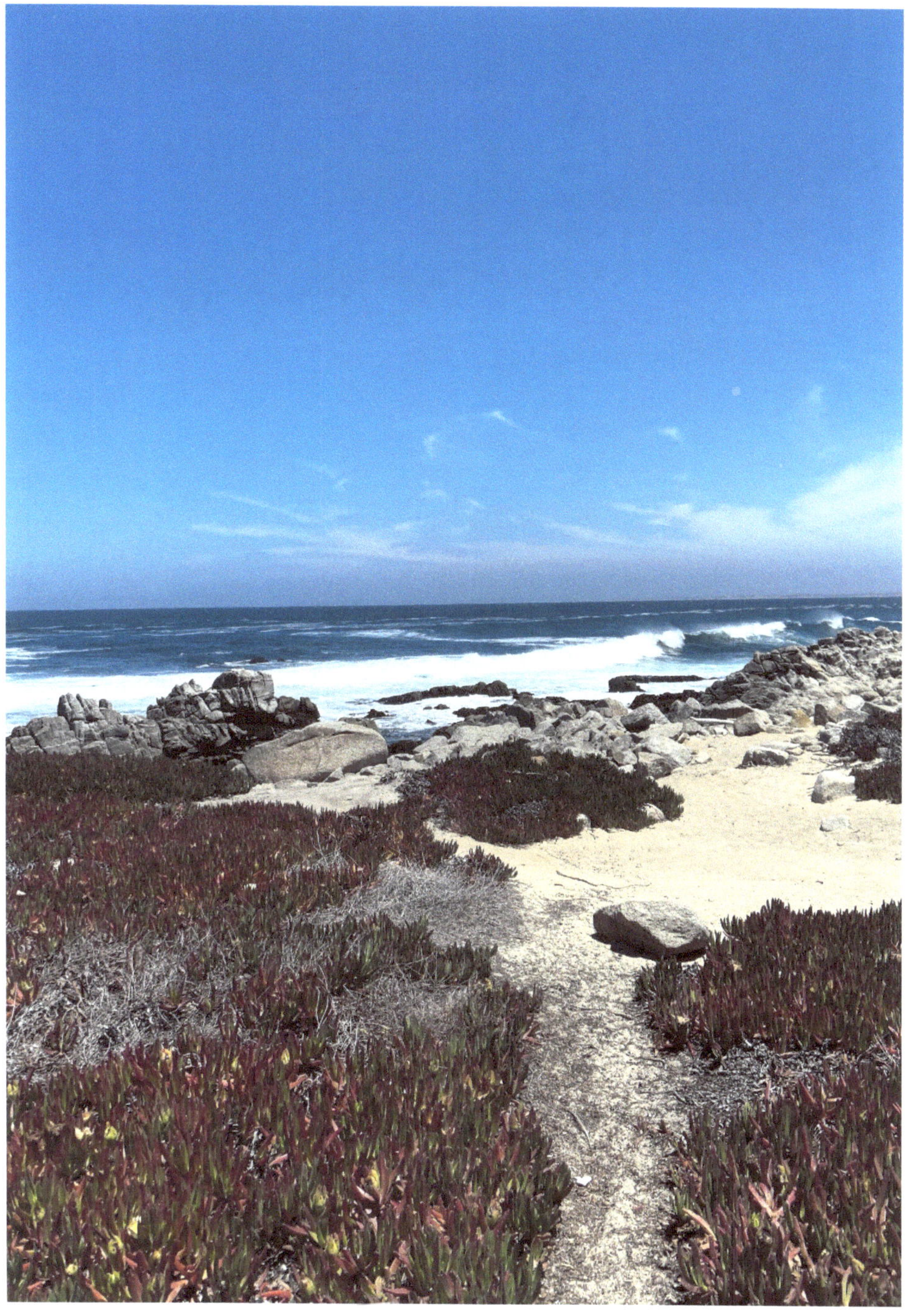

and the worry presses to meet goals while time remains.

Then one reaches a blissful place in time.

The measuring stick is replaced by

Self-awareness and confidence.

Now time may stand still or pass slowly.

When you reach this place

you may be tempted to linger in reverie.

Perhaps awaken in a dream moment

surrounded by a sleepy hue,

with lingering thoughts

that whisper of frogs leaping lily pods in youthful anticipation.

Linger as long as you dare, but be aware

that time continues to pass outside your youthful cocoon.

You cannot go back.

You cannot relive the time past.

If you try through regret

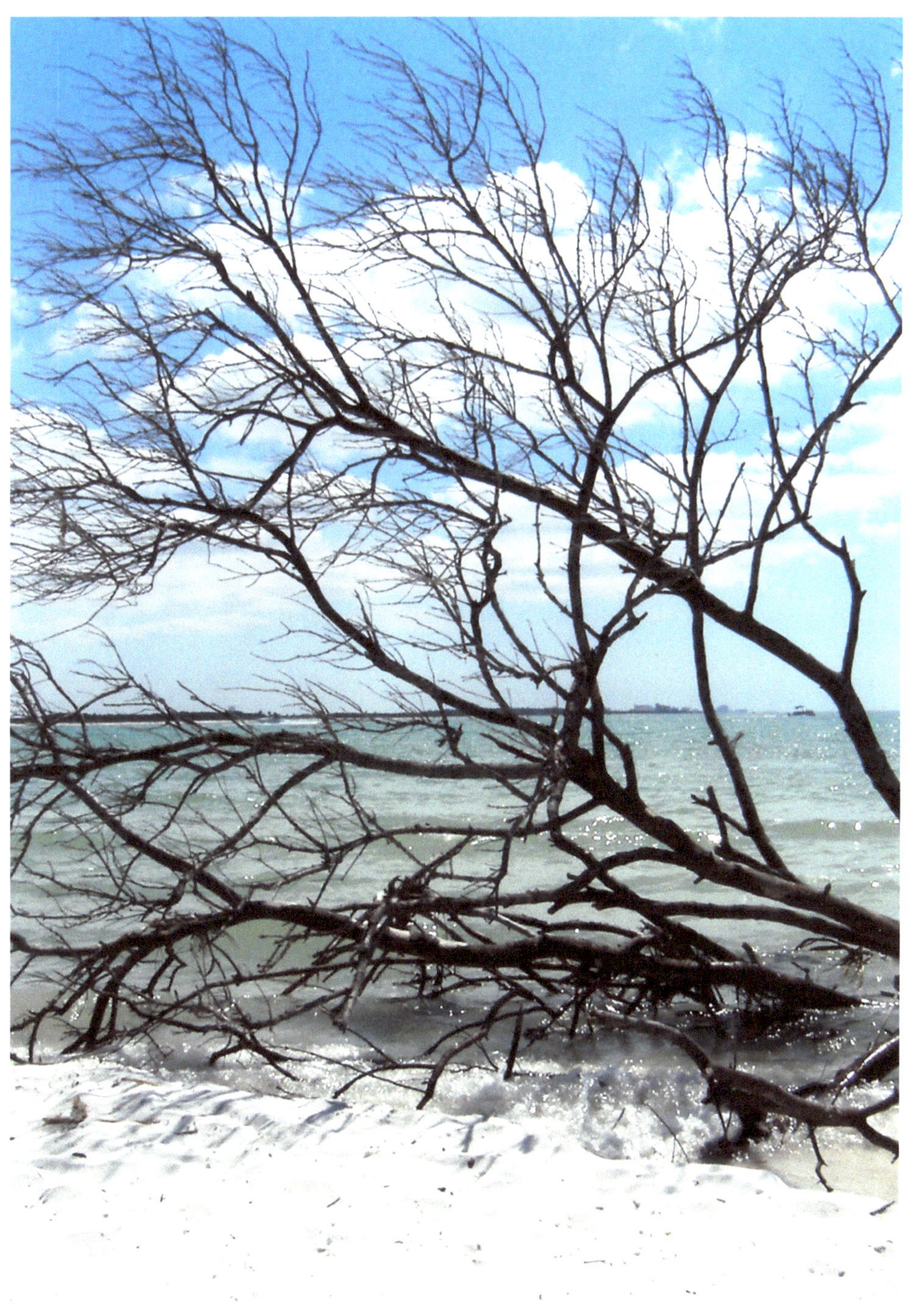

time will only pass more quickly.

You may not notice

until the day when the transition begins.

The dream state will begin to shift.

Find something real to measure.

If you refuse to accept your place in time,

if you continue to scan the sky,

playfully plucking at the shapes of clouds like a child,

eventually you will be aware that you cannot let go.

You will also be aware that you cannot stay.

All that is left is to accept your fate or

waste away another day in echoes of yesterday's bliss.

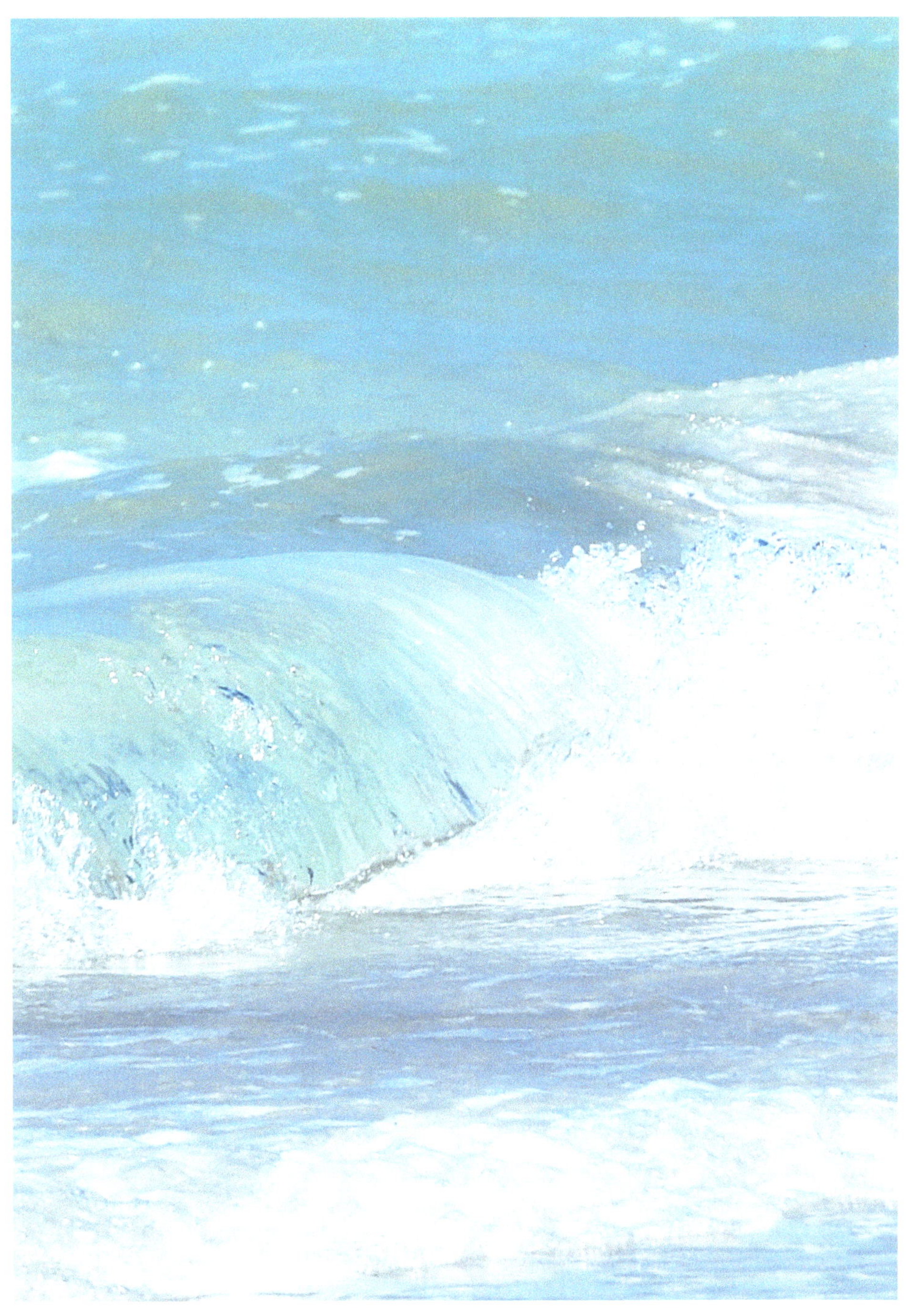

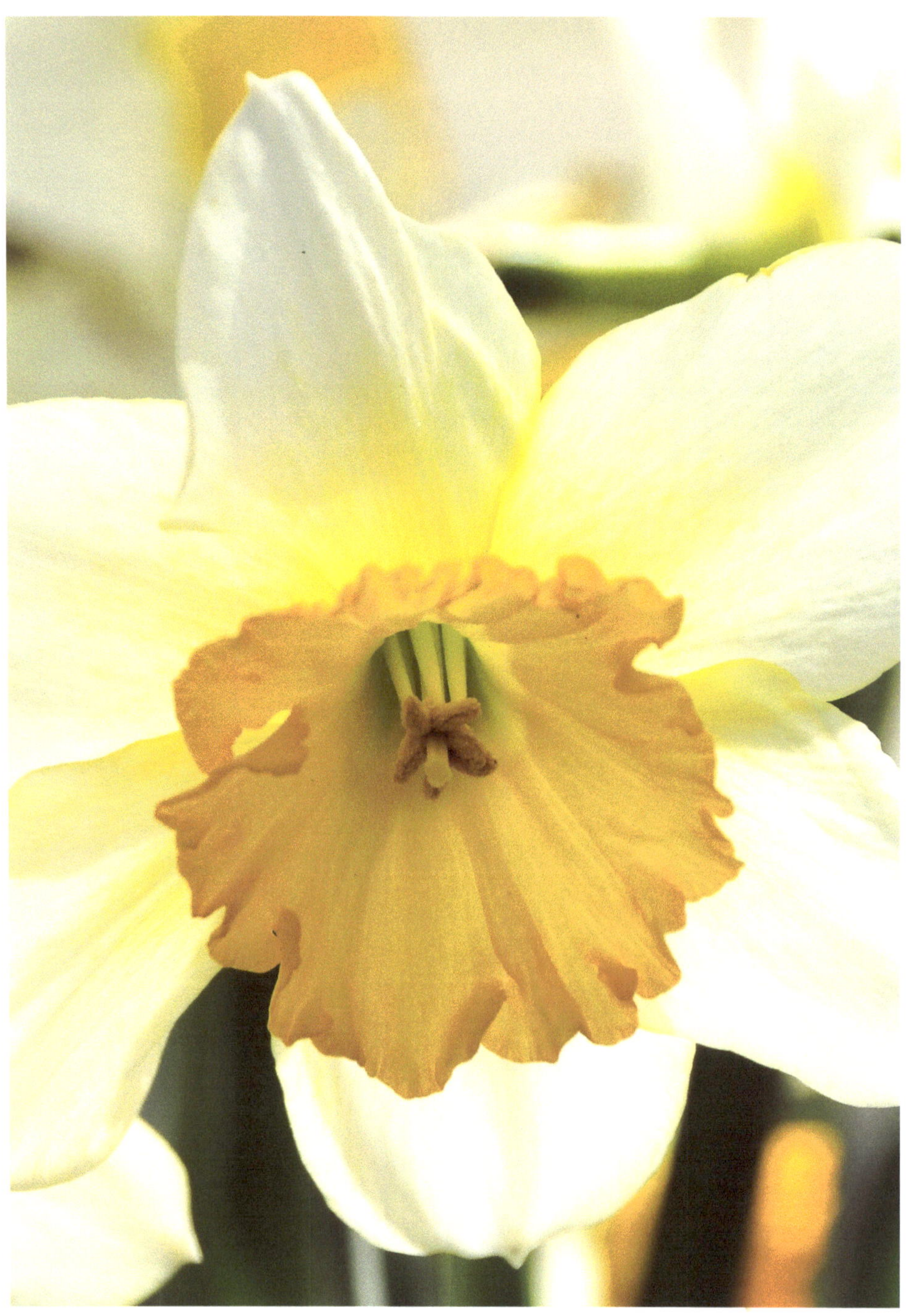

Spring Blossoms

They are like a fetus in the mother's womb,
nurtured from the rich dark soil
heavy with rain.
While stretching their spreading roots
growing deep and wide across the land.
These flowers appear like phantoms,
quietly, in the last hours of the night.
They whisper their sweet scents
like secrets revealed
on a warm soft breeze.
They are sometimes captured for display
or admiration, rarely gone unnoticed
for their beauty.
They are first to arrive in Spring,
reminders of hope and new beginnings.

They are Mother nature's gifts

and represent her new yearly cycle.

A fresh start to all that is possible.

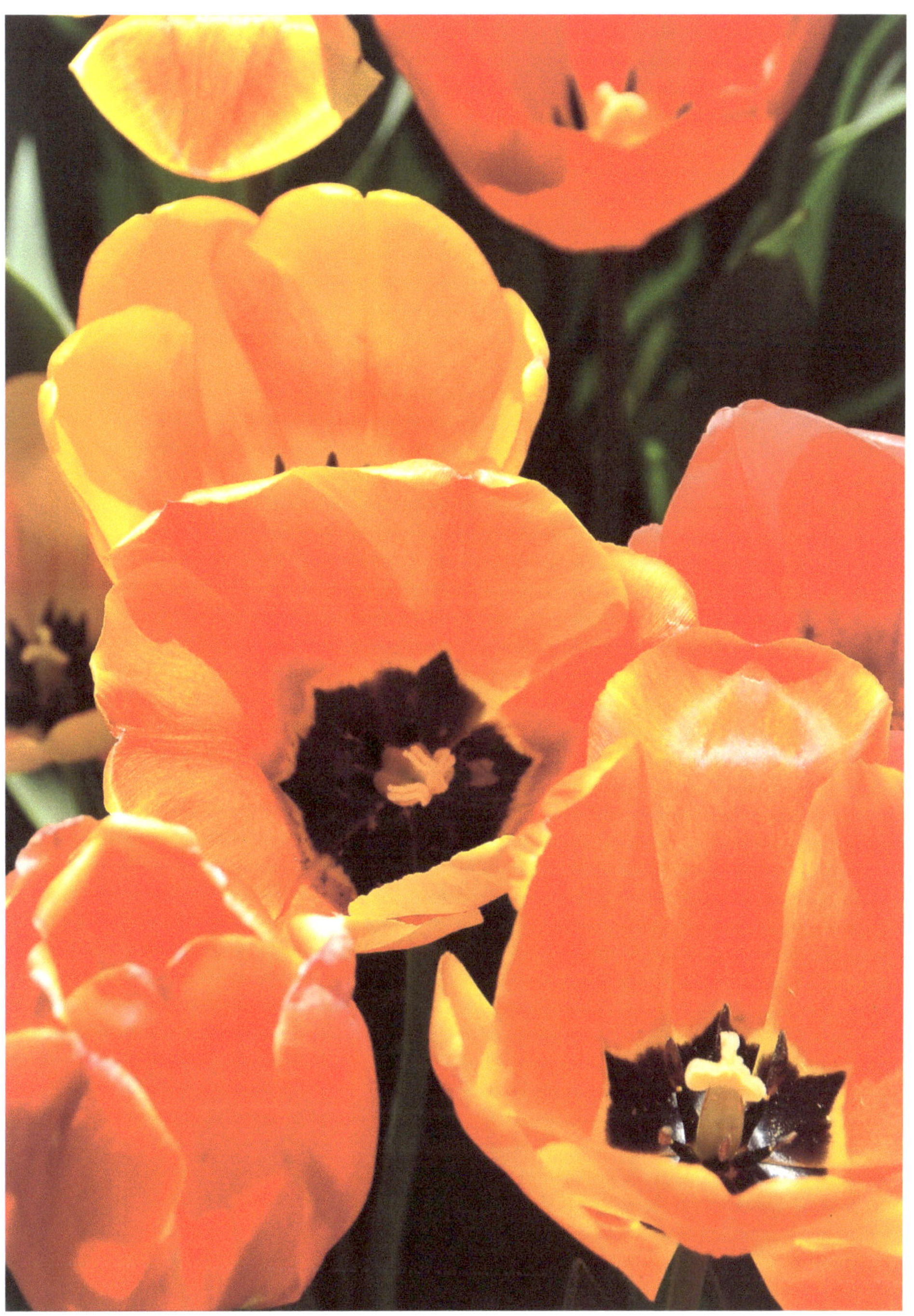

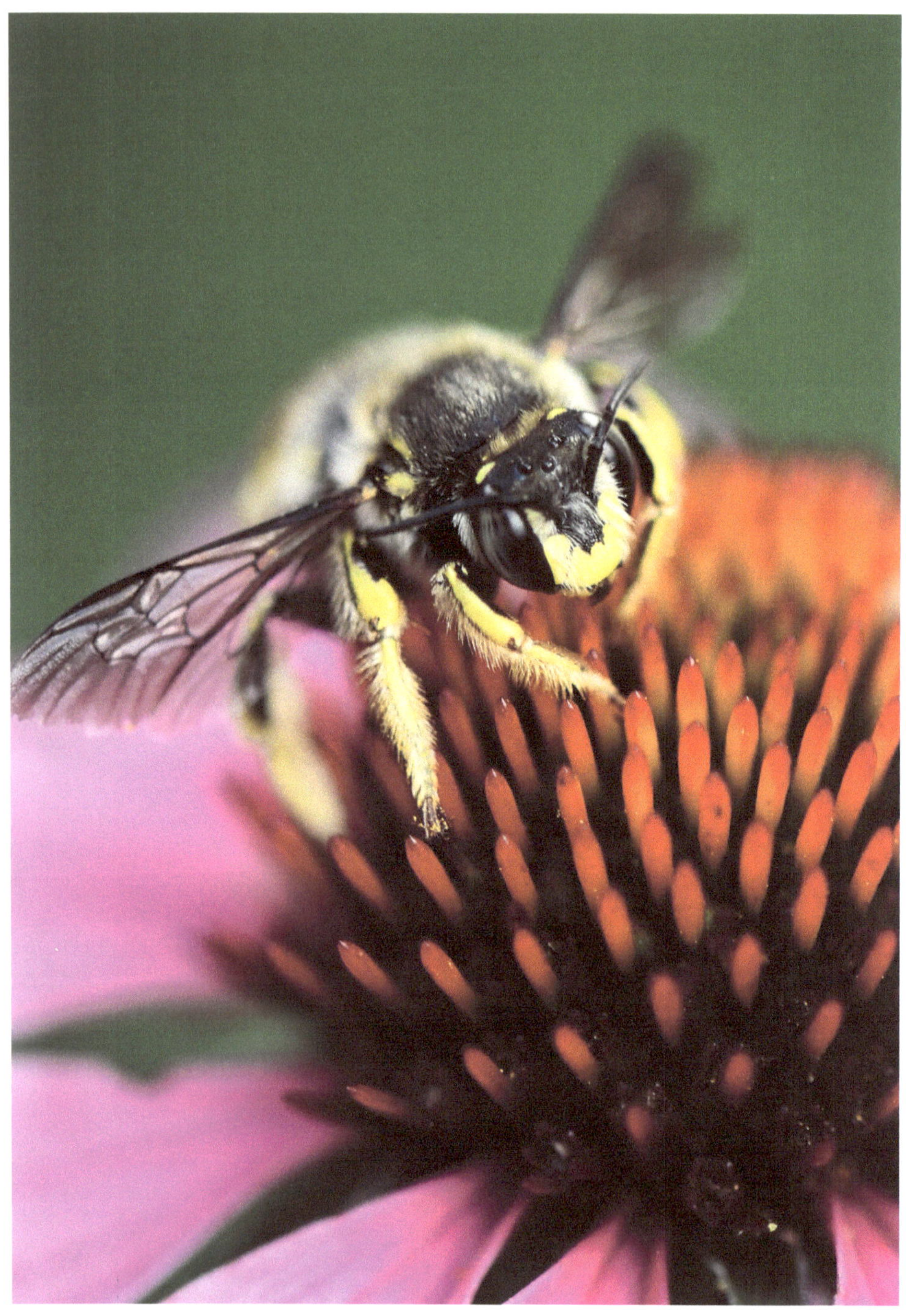

The Dance

A chance encounter is the very best way

for the dance to begin.

From across a crowded and loud watering hole

their eyes first met and he held her gaze.

Truth be told he took her breath away.

Oh, I am in trouble now she told herself.

This man is already wielding a heavy sword

of charm in my direction.

When he approached she tried a coy smile

but he was too self-confident for that.

He swayed next to her, close enough

for her to smell him and his scent was intoxicating.

He flashed a huge smile and introduced himself

while at the same time saying he had to leave

because there was a dog in his truck waiting.

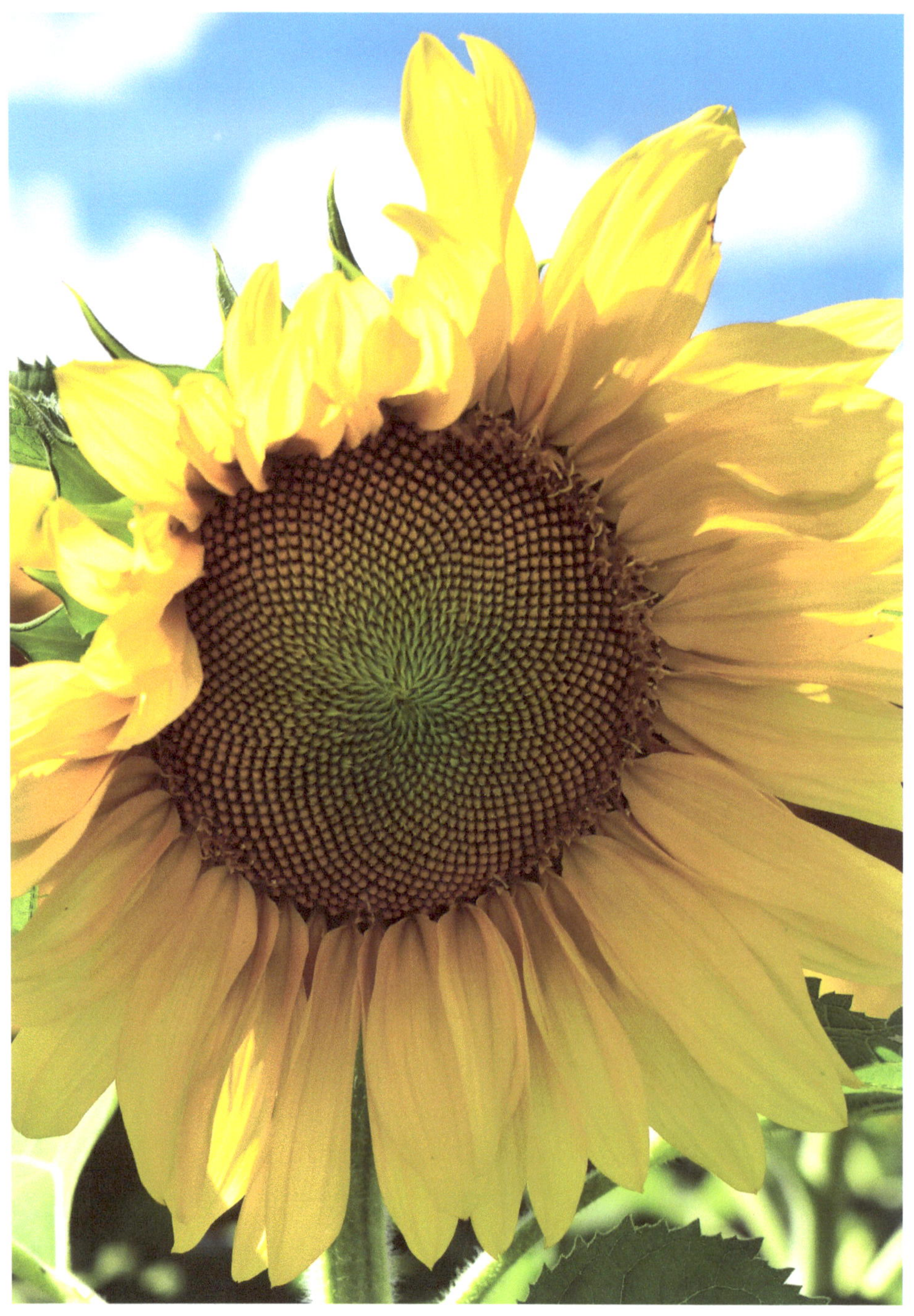

He handed her a business card, said, "call me" and left.

She was struck by how confident he was,

by how handsome he was and

by the way he smelled.

She did not call, and the dance continued.

On another night weeks later

at that same watering hole

he came up from behind her

and gently placed his hand on the small of her back.

A welcome surprise in the smoky room,

the touch of his hand on her back was

familiar somehow, as if it belonged there.

The small talk conversation turned into

a plan of introduction, the first of many,

each a further validation

that they were meant to be together.

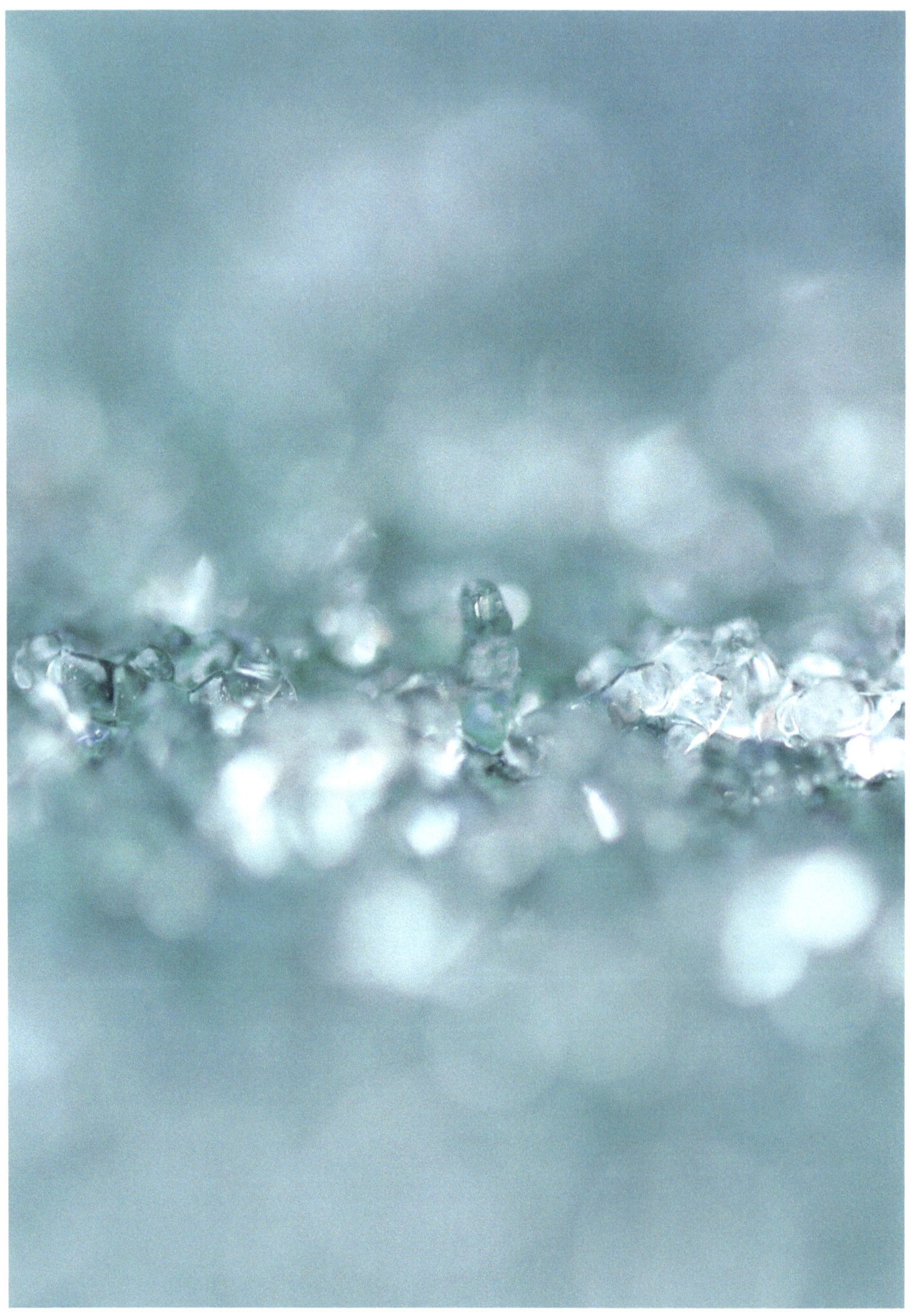

His best friends gave her a photograph
that reinforced her excitement
every time she pulled it out to take a look.
It was almost as if having that picture
was some physical proof of the feelings
growing quickly within.
The moment she knew she had fallen was
not during any of the shared late night
dinners, or during a midnight swim,
or while at Sunday beach volleyball play,
or while fishing out on the open ocean,
or even while exploring intimacy.
The exact moment she knew she was his
was on the dance floor while in his arms.
Together they did trip that light.
Their dance continued

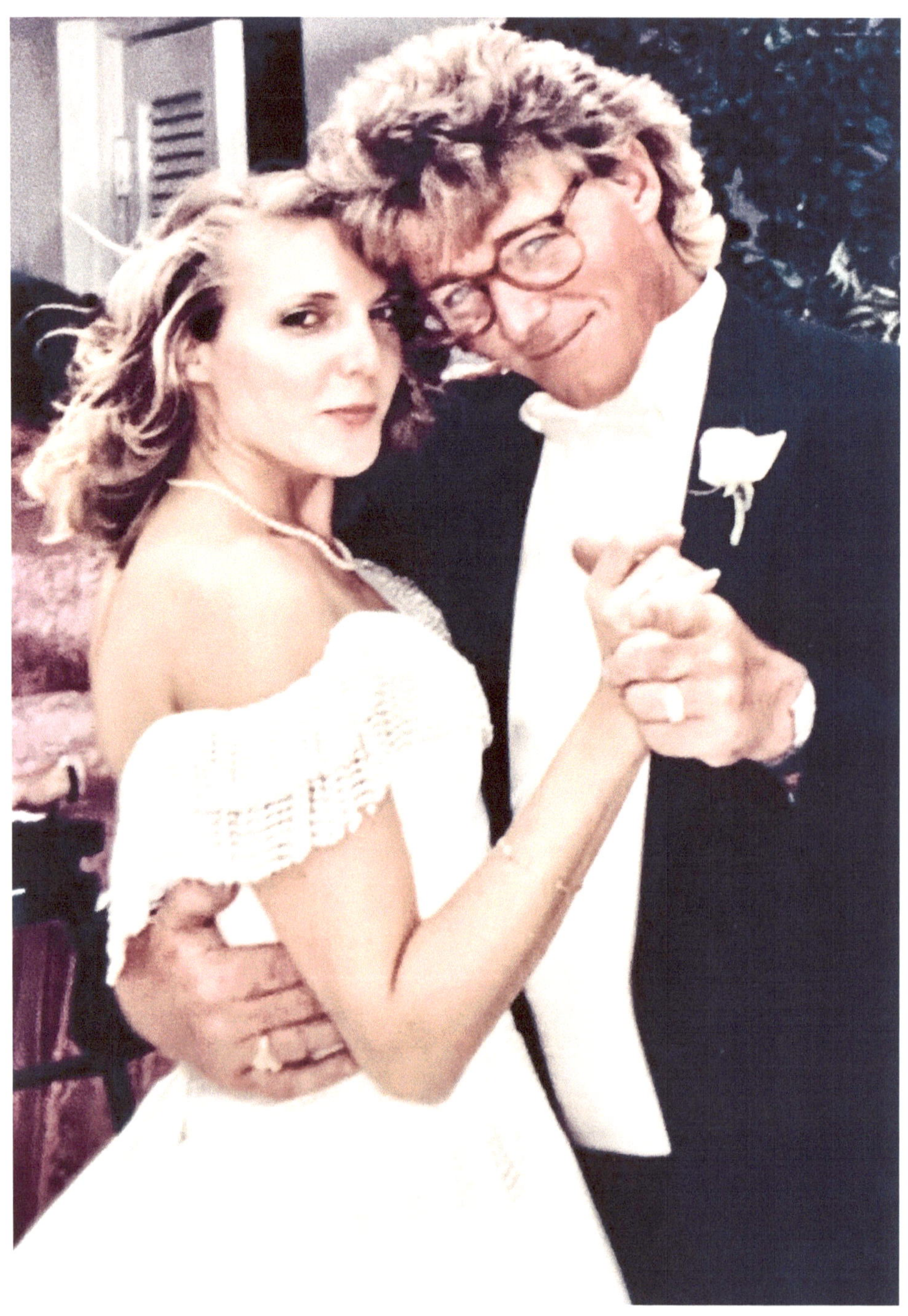

all through the social season.

When the New Year came without engagement

a challenge presented.

"If you are not going to marry her I will a friend said"

and they all laughed.

Not long after, the same Merle the dog

left waiting in the truck the night they met

came walking up to her

with a smile on his tricolor face

and a small package around his neck.

They twirled forward in their dance

when she said yes

to the question never asked.

Glass Ceiling

Before she earned her college degree

she had come to understand

that the best place to work,

the place with the most likelihood of success for women

was in the finance industry.

At a time when Corporate America

was driven by old men in sloppy suits

and their sons with sharp tongues

who had not yet learned to tie their own ties,

there were women bank managers.

Women were on the rise in banking.

They held high and mid-level positions

in origination lending and servicing,

with some even skirting the executive level.

So there she began a corporate career

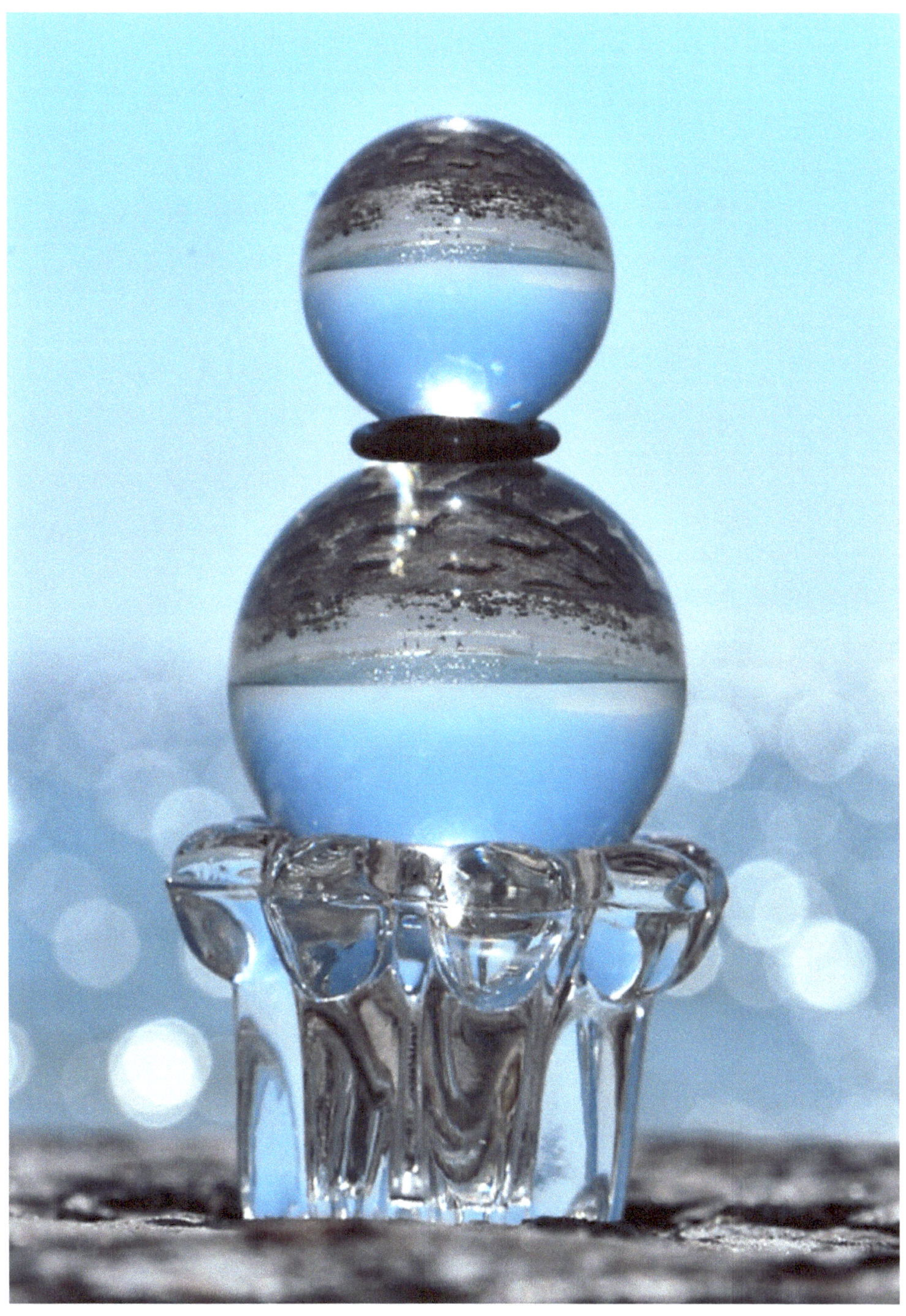

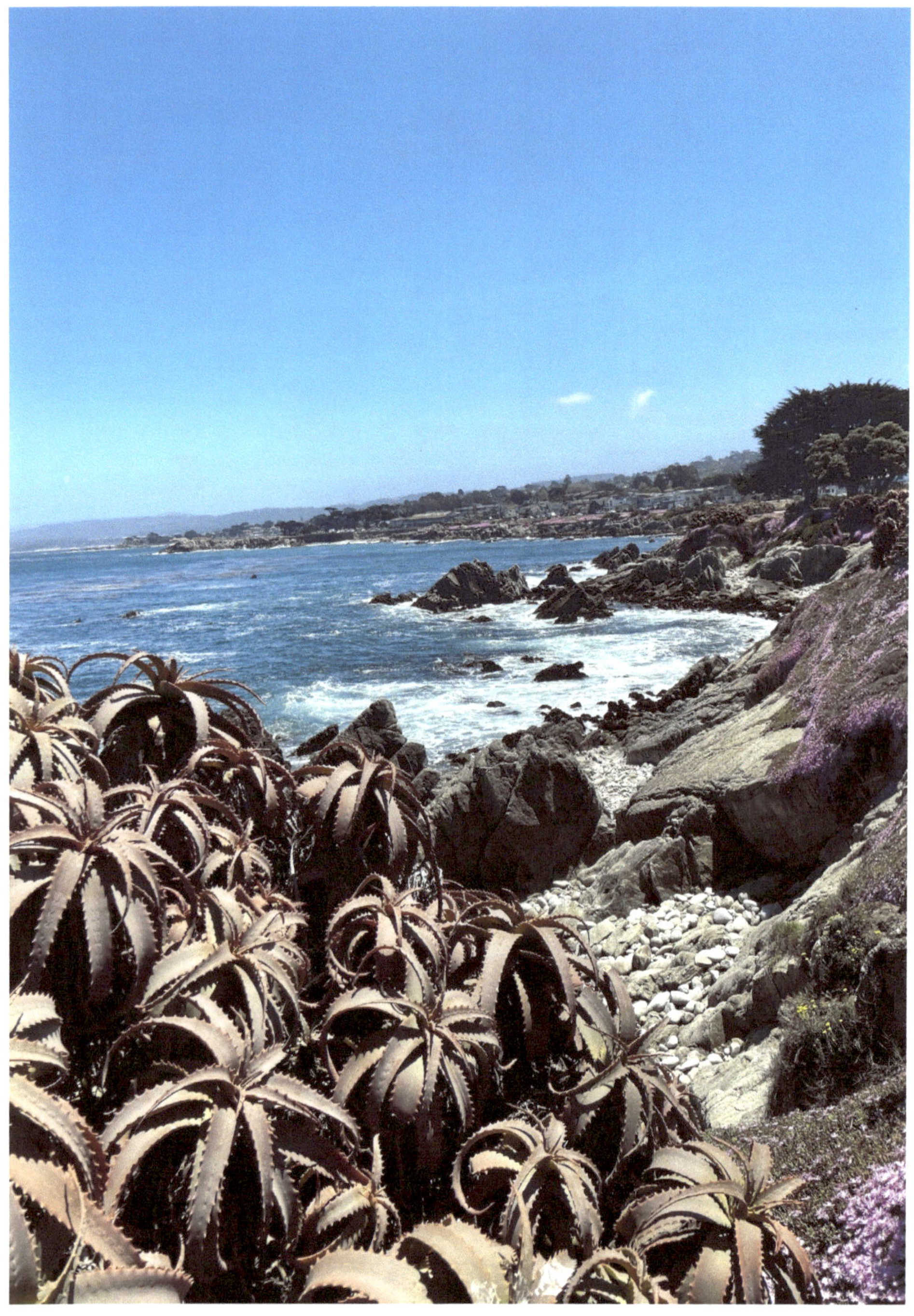

She had enough business experience to get through the door,

and the endurance it took to stay.

So she stayed, waiting patiently for the right time

when a lead promotion dangled within her grasp.

She was the most ready.

She had the best performance.

She would have won the position if not for

that she was about to become a new mother.

It was a wonder anything was said at all.

If it happened 35 years later

there would have been consequences.

The only comment made - perhaps in condolence

was a comment from the deciding manager, her manager,

saying he assumed she would quit after the baby came.

She wanted to scream,

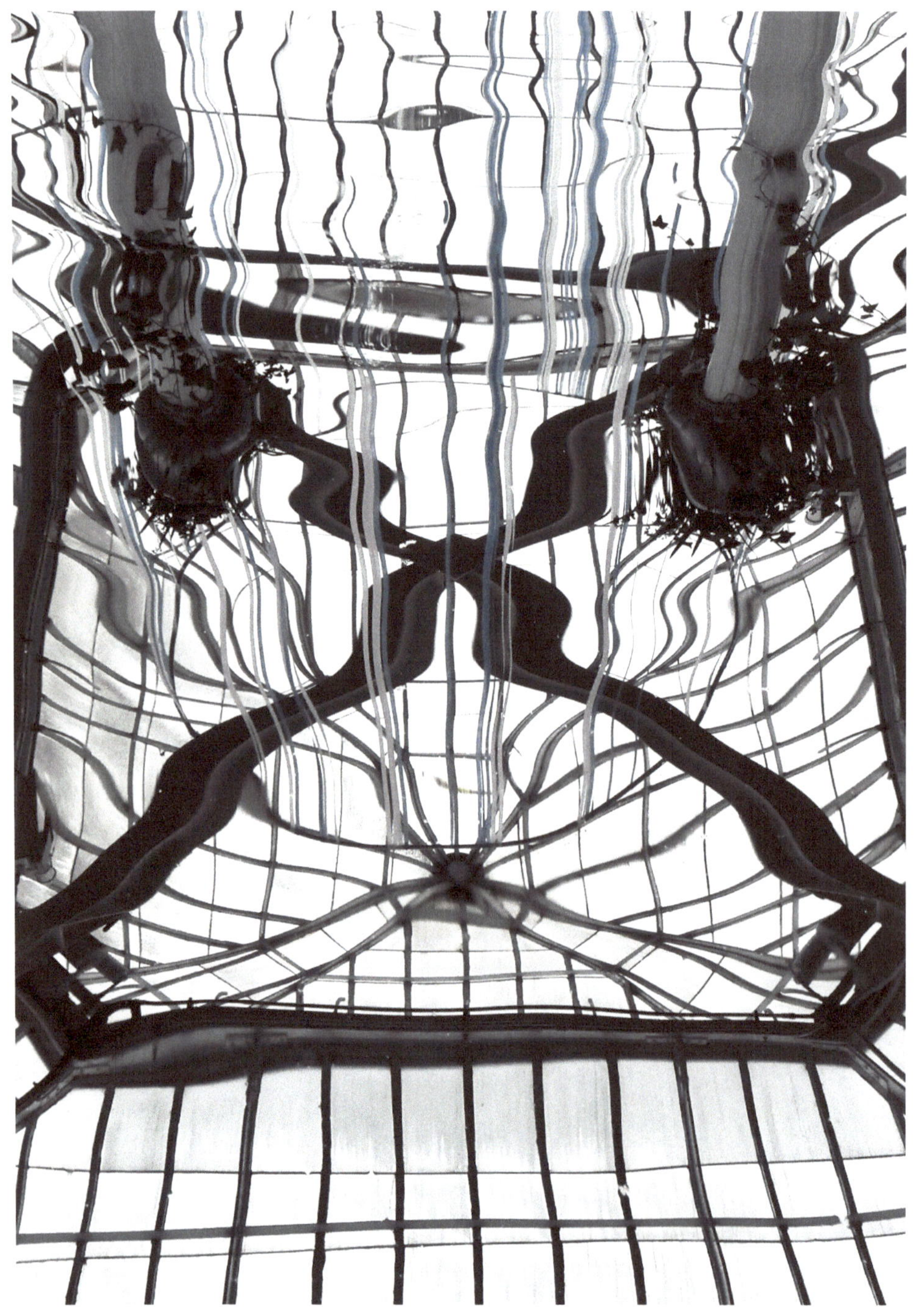

YOU CHAUVINISTIC JERK!

Instead she stood stunned in silence.

She considered leaving

but quitting at that time was not a real option.

The day after giving birth,

and while still in her hospital bed,

she continued to make it rain.

When she returned to the office

it was difficult to see any future there,

or any possibility of rising higher

beyond the glass ceiling

now covered in a murky glaze.

Child Birth

Today is the day.

I am not sure how I know,

I just do.

I know and I am ready.

So I go about my business as if

this is just another ordinary day; as if

I will be surprised somehow; as if

I could forget that I know.

I exercise, I cook, and I red up rooms.

I tell him to shower.

He obeys without question.

It's almost as though he knows too.

Off we go.

With us we carry our special music,

my overnight bag, a small cooler filled

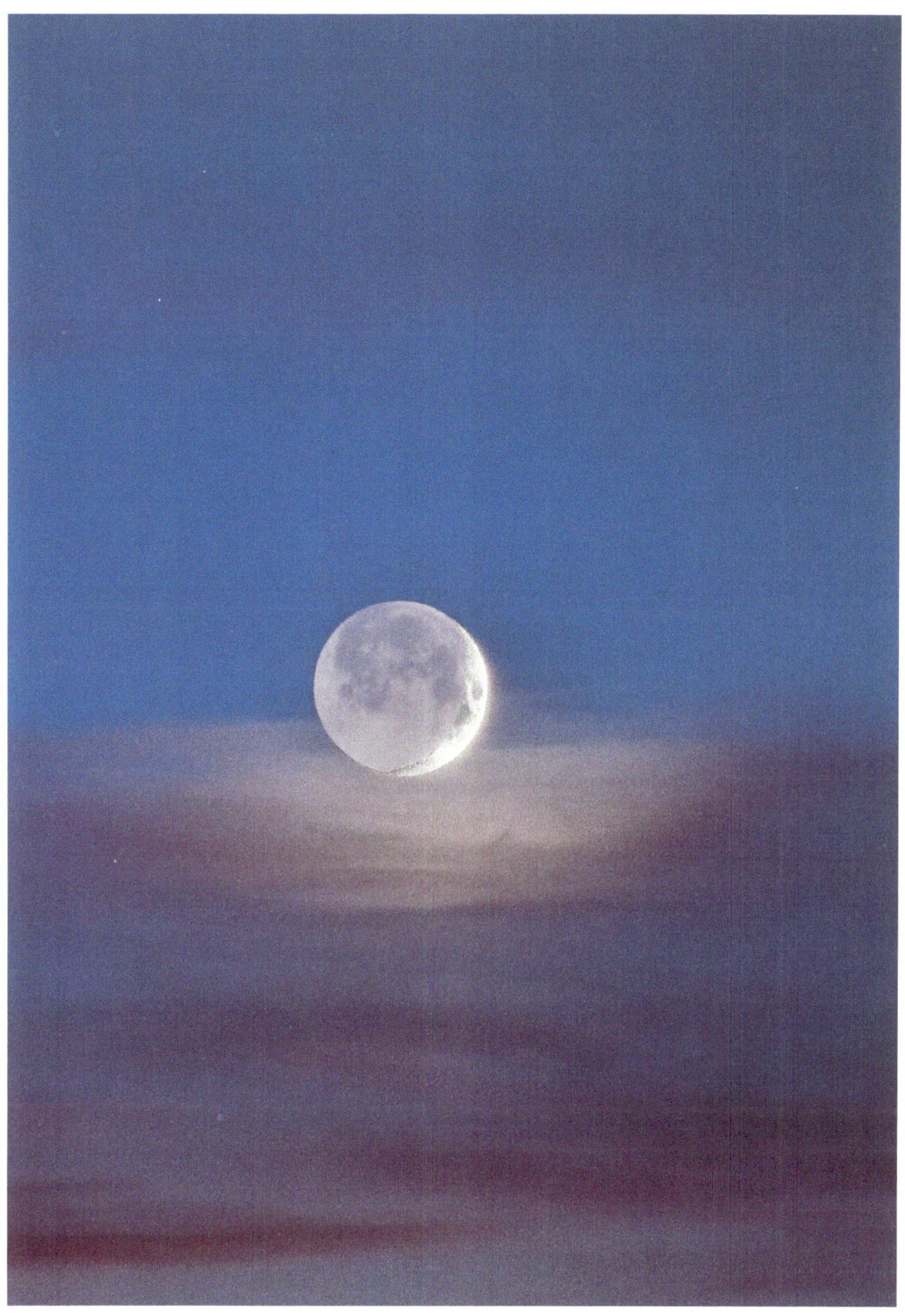

with popsicles, and our excitement.

Upon arrival we find ourselves

in an unanticipated competition

for the birthing suite.

We are one of several couples in labor.

At first we were like anxious gamers

playing against the clock.

Soon that all melted away

as did the popsicles in the cooler.

We turned into monitor watchers.

We watched the rise and fall of each new contraction.

It was boring after the first hour and we fell asleep on and off.

Time seemed to stand still.

Then suddenly, without any real warning,

time moved fast-forward

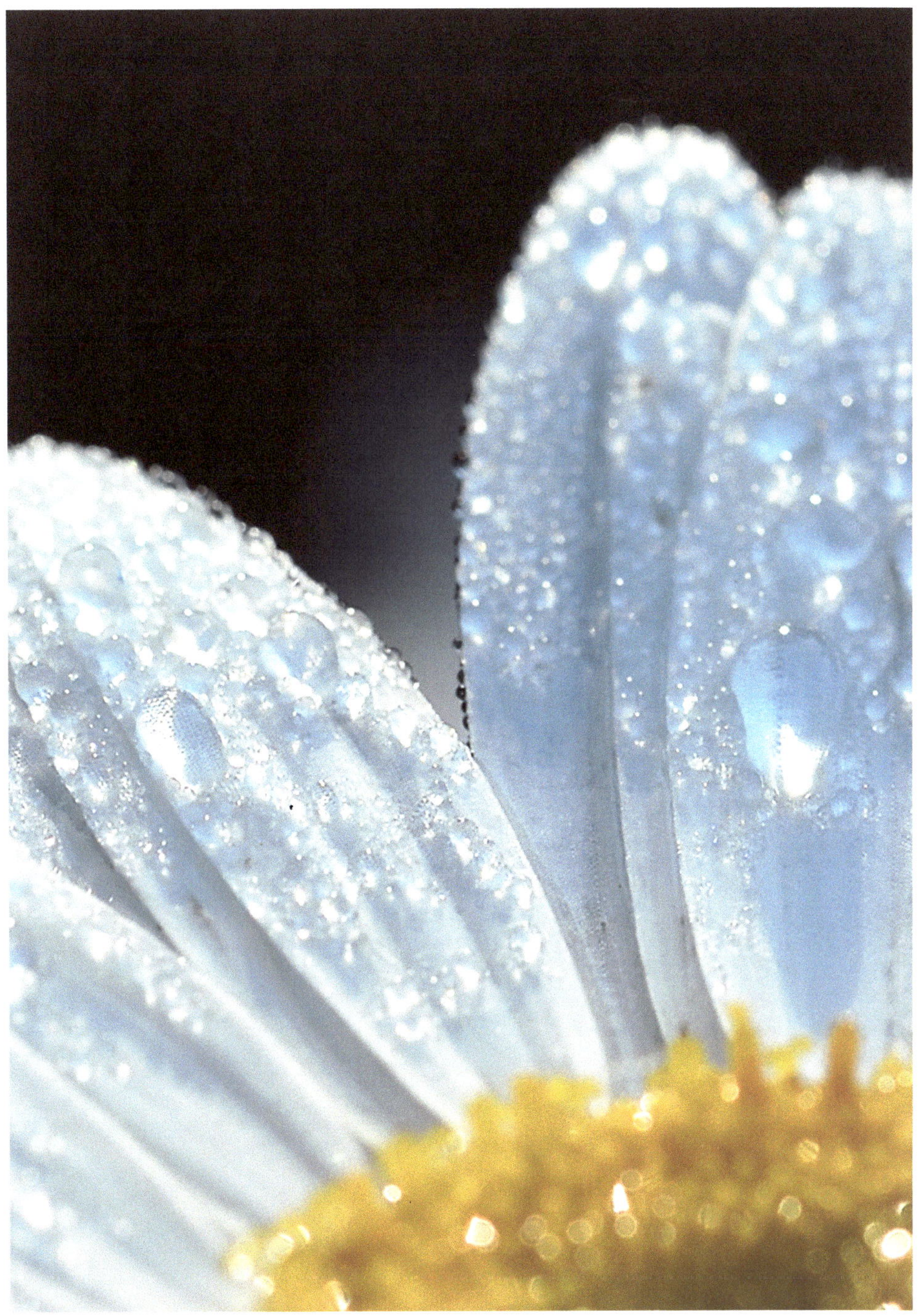

through transition-too fast to control the water break,

as if that's even possible.

Too fast for him to find his shoes.

Too fast for the birthing suite.

The baby had already moved through the birth canal,

like a Navy Seal.

The Doctor had not arrived

so they told me not to push.

If I had known baby's head was fully

birthed I would not have tried to stop.

No matter because

this baby refused to wait another minute.

Without one small effort baby was free.

The she we did not know.

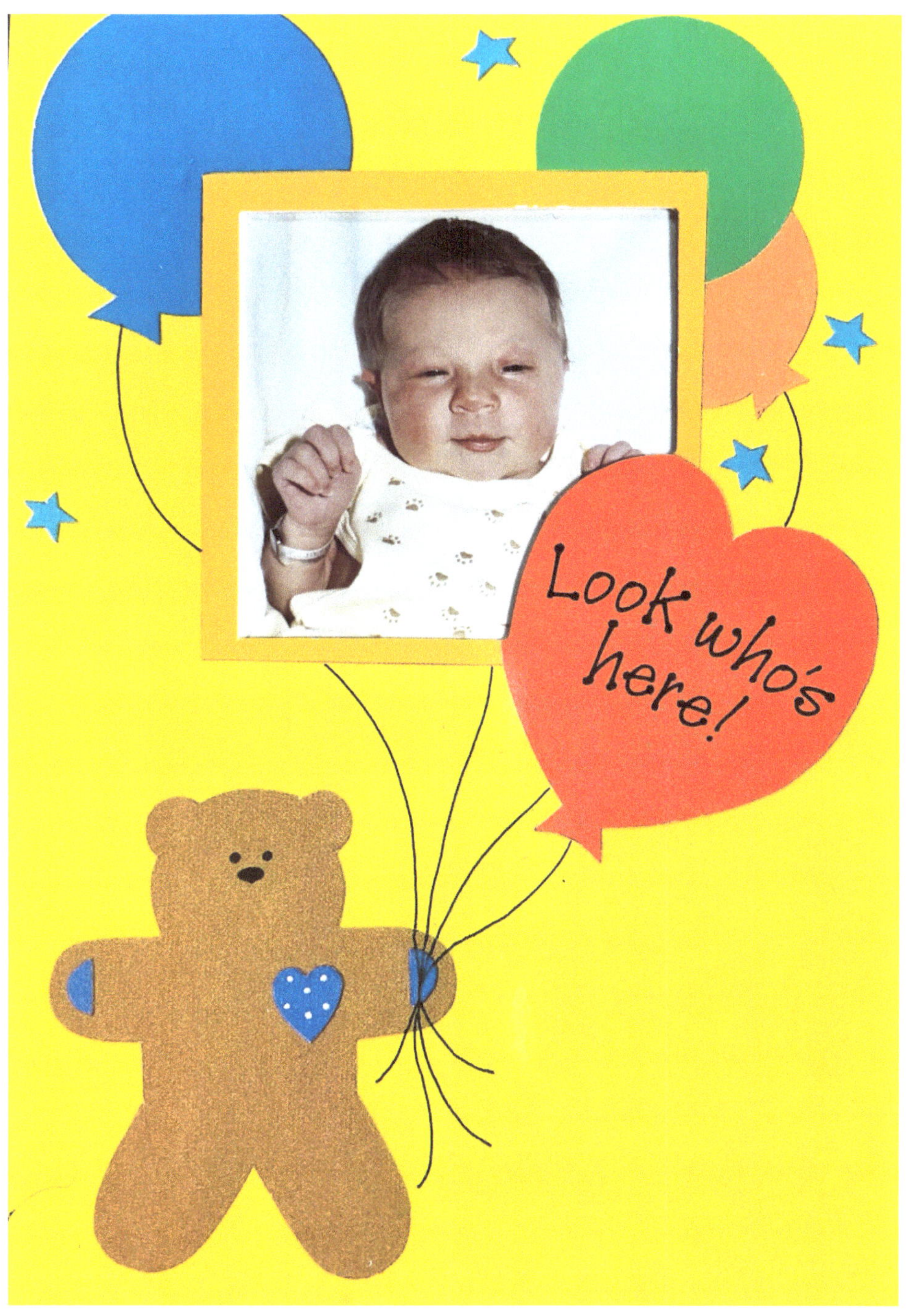
Look who's here!

Hindsight

Back at the crossroads.

Ready to move on, again.

It's still the same full circle.

Some things will never change.

Only faces differ,

circumstance of change.

The heart aches lonely

with the intensity of a rain,

that falls lightly,

unnoticed,

but nagging all the same.

While life moves forward

one may slip away from the pain,

memories of the all time spent

freely echoes to remain

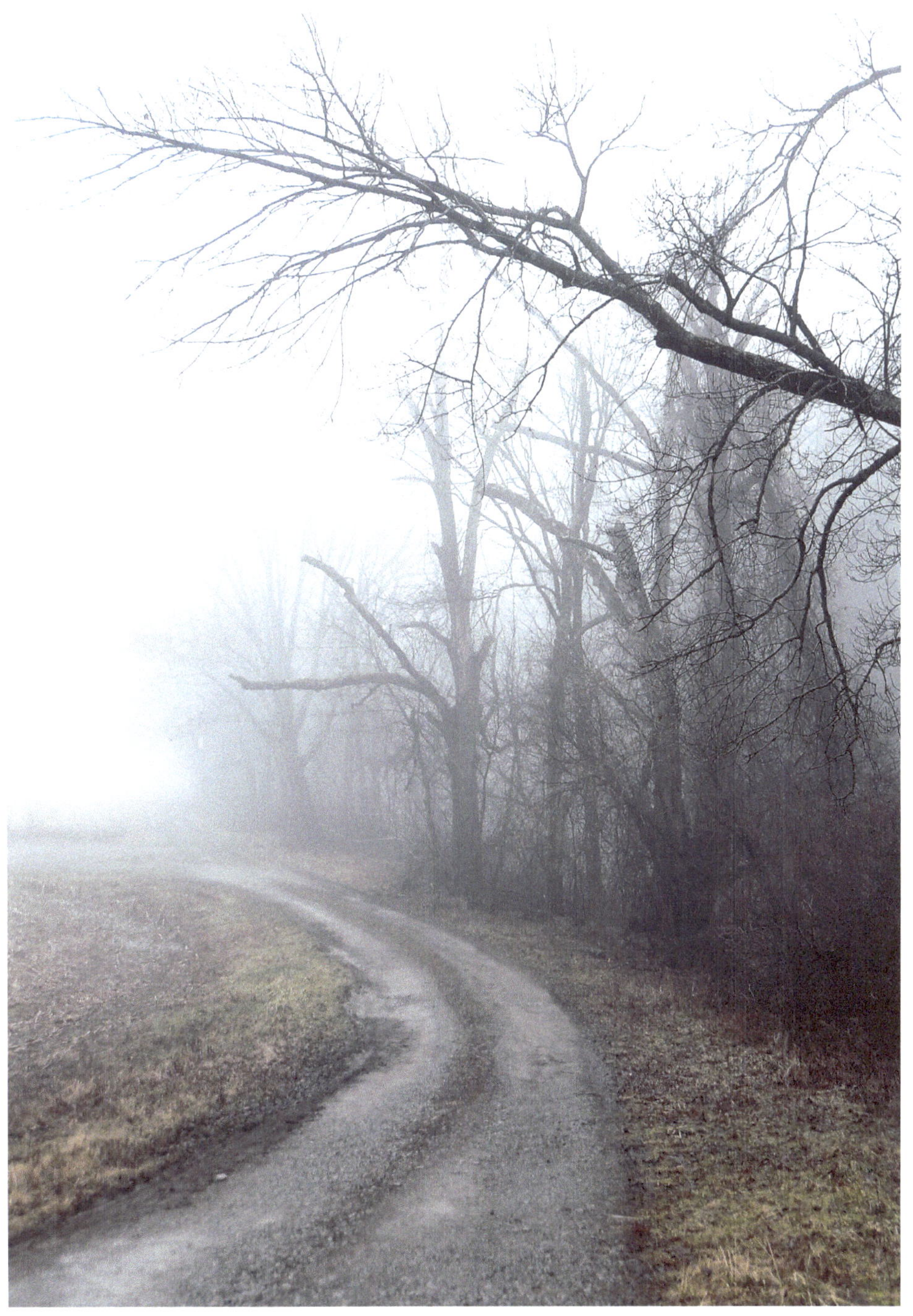

through the tunnels of your mind.

Like your vision when narrowed and blind,

it would be so unkind to say

that it did not mean much anyway.

It did not mean much anyway.

Still the mind as gatekeeper

finds a word or song powerful enough

to revive those pictures left behind.

Like a worn out cliche, so familiar

to replay as if for the first time.

As if you can find solace in what other people say.

As if it all didn't mean much anyway.

It didn't mean much anyway.

So on it goes.

You are searching for contentment

in what you believe everyone else knows.

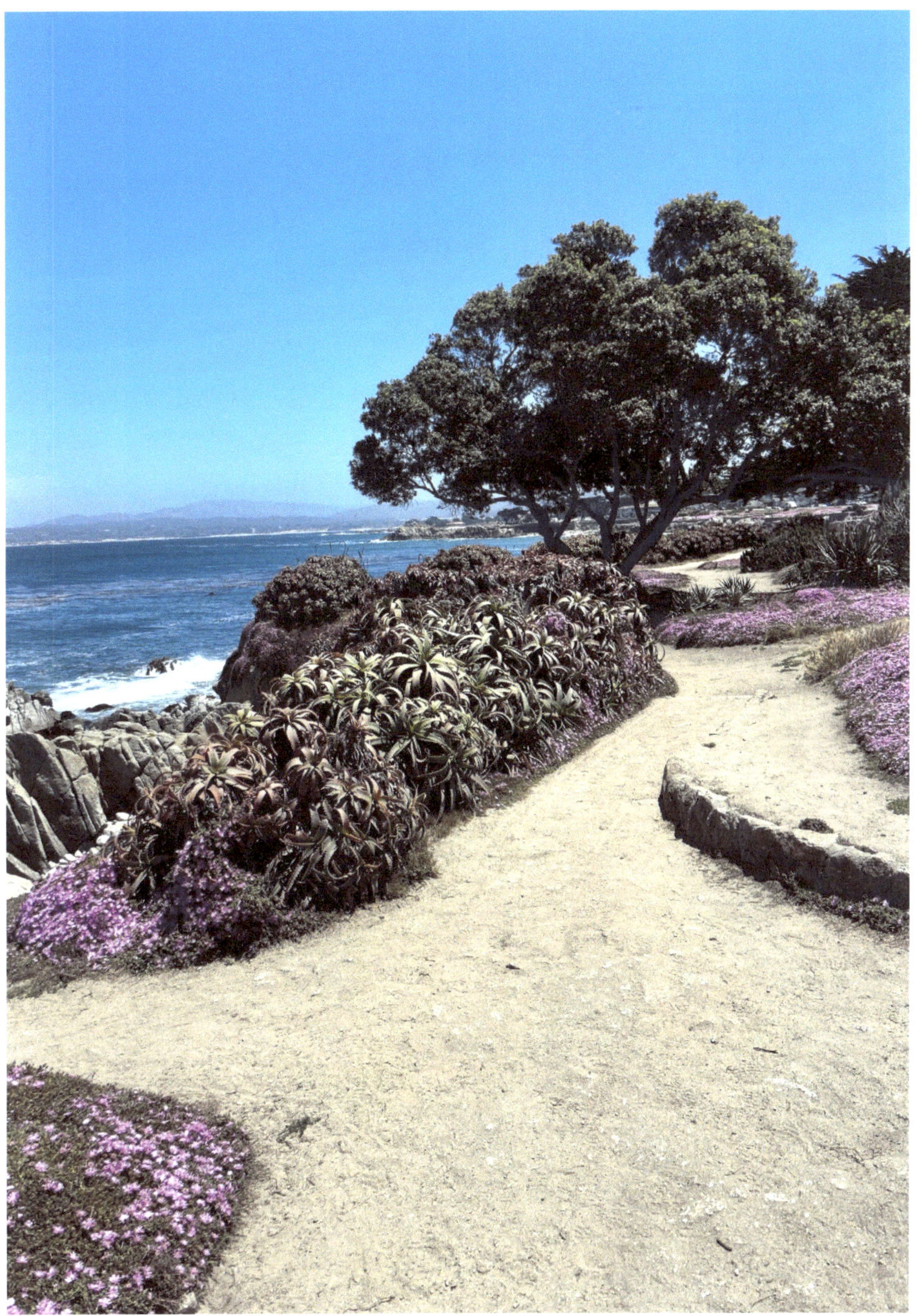

You are left a prisoner of their clues.

When all the truth you need, the key

to set you free

is the acceptance

of your truth.

The only truth to know alone along the way.

The rest doesn't mean much anyway.

It really doesn't mean much anyway.

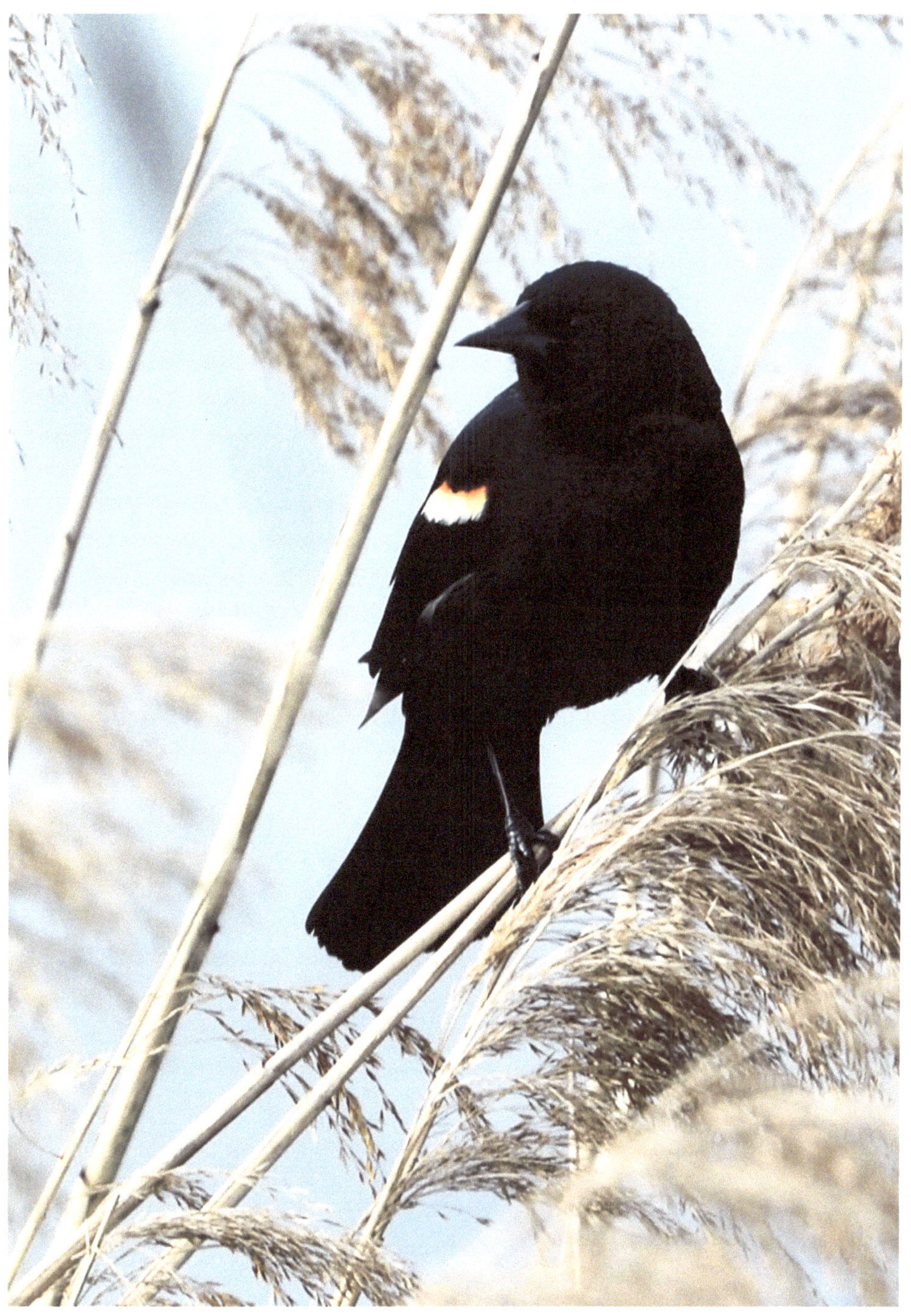

Out of the Nest

Each milestone along the way
I was preparing for that day.
Each year for eighteen years.
Each milestone along the way
I was more self-assured that all the
decisions I made were the right ones,
though some were not perfect.
Each milestone along the way
there was laughter, tears,
and sometimes frustration.
Each milestone along the way
I found myself filled with pride
and wonder at the kind person
you grew to be.

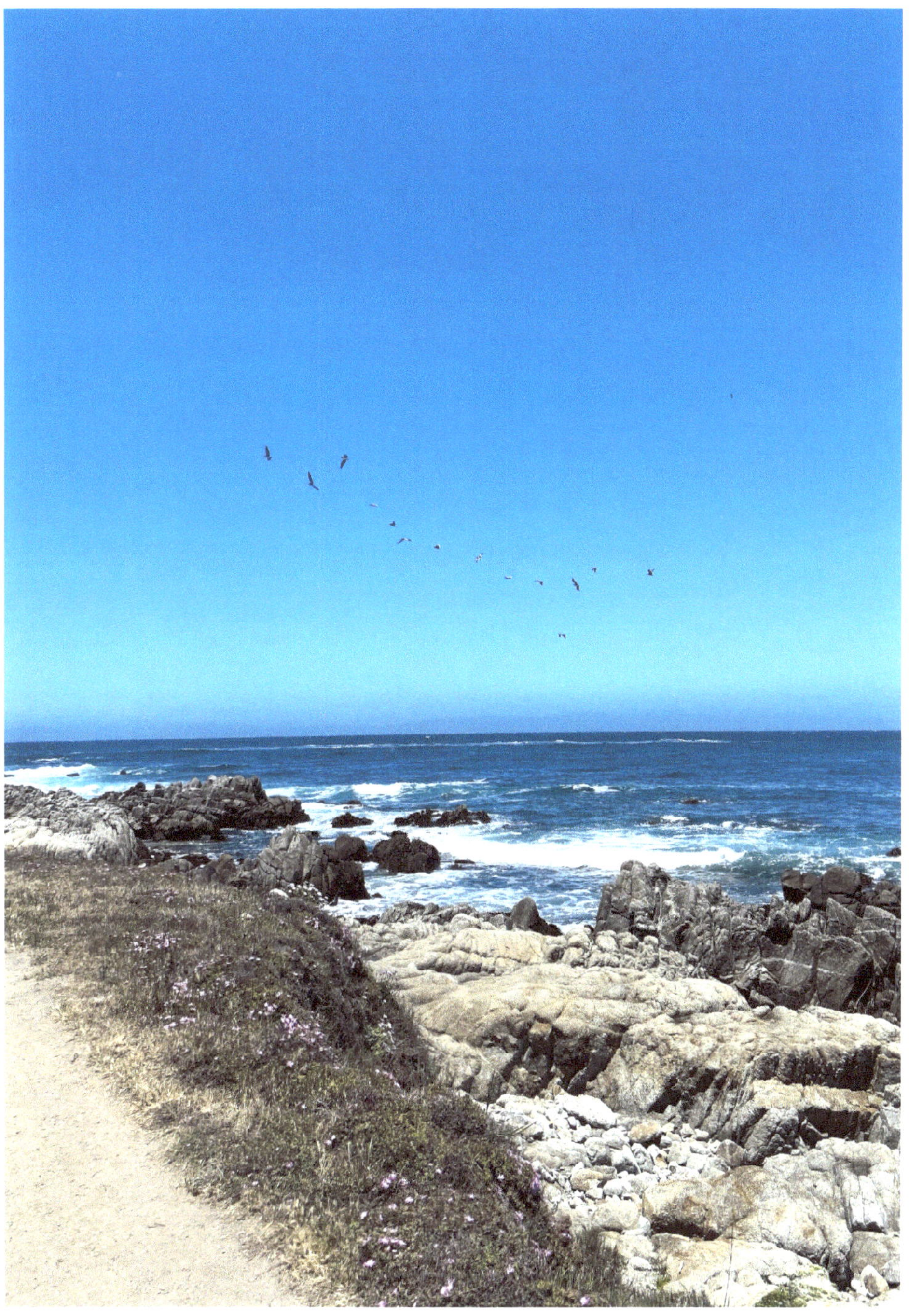

Each milestone along the way
I forgot that this day would come
because I was too busy
with all the things
that filled up all the days before.
Each milestone along the way
I found it harder to witness
the growing pains, each more serious
than the one before.
Each milestone along the way
I wanted to shelter you
but I knew that was not possible.
Each milestone along the way
I tried not to interfere but
I know that sometimes I did.

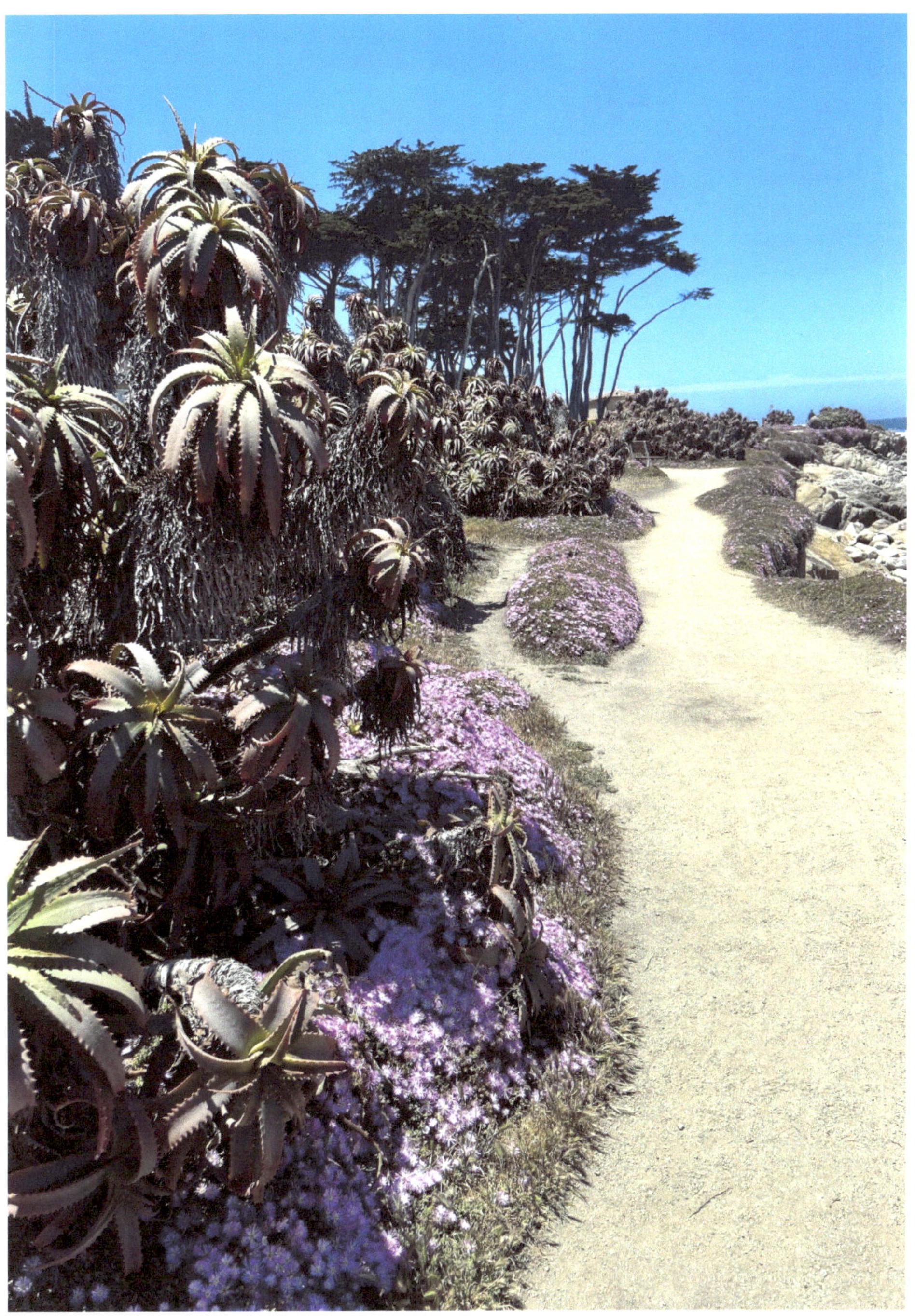

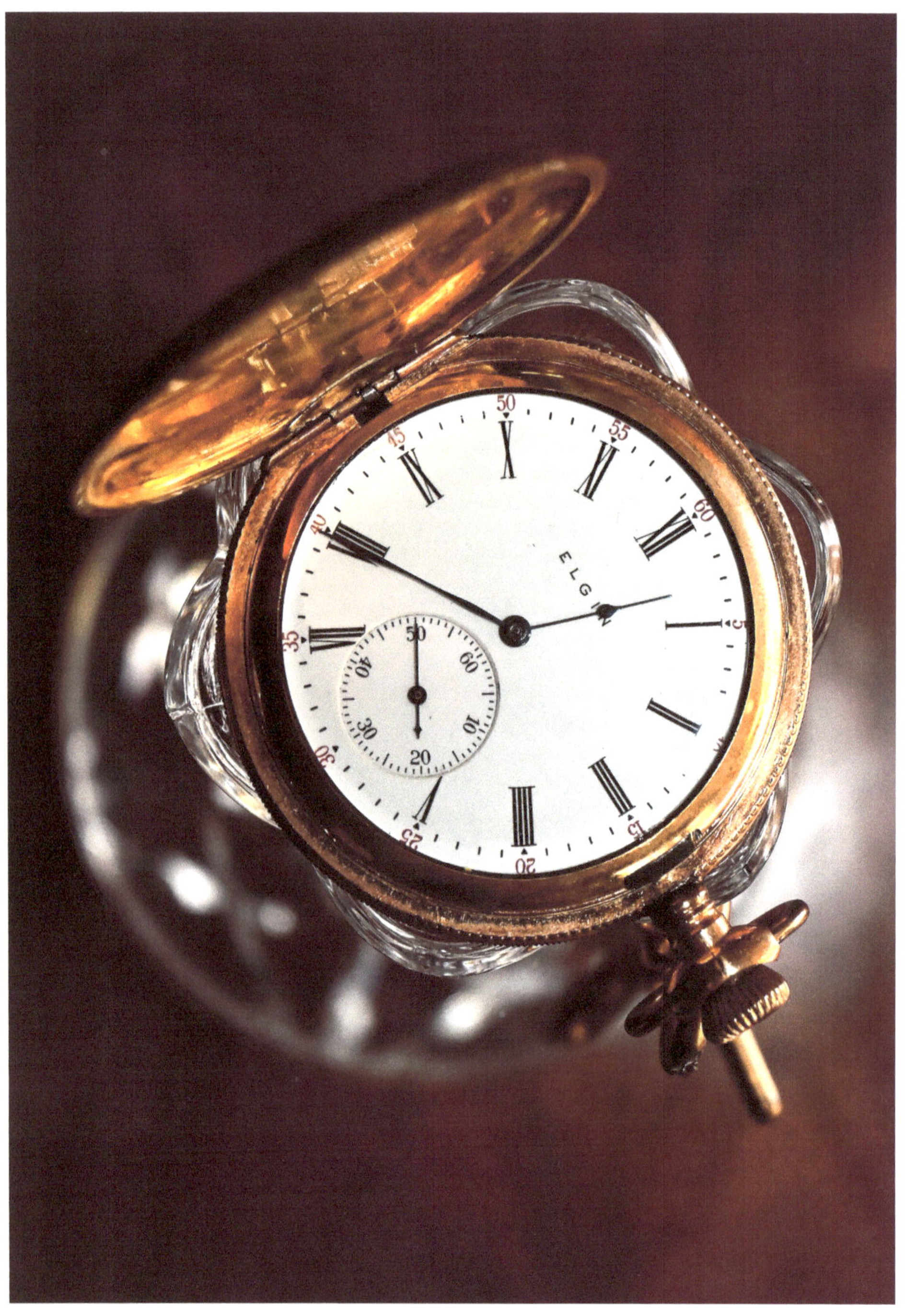

Each milestone along the way
I wanted to stay close, to share, to be
the only one you confided in;
but I knew that you could not.
Each milestone along the way
I tried my best to understand
what you were experiencing.
I tried to remember how I must have felt
all those years ago.
But I knew that was not practical.
Each milestone along the way
I became more fearful
of the inevitable day that I would lose you.
That day did come.
You stood ready with your decision made.
You stood strong and independent.

Though I was already filling with regret,

I knew you had reached the milestone

for that I had prepared.

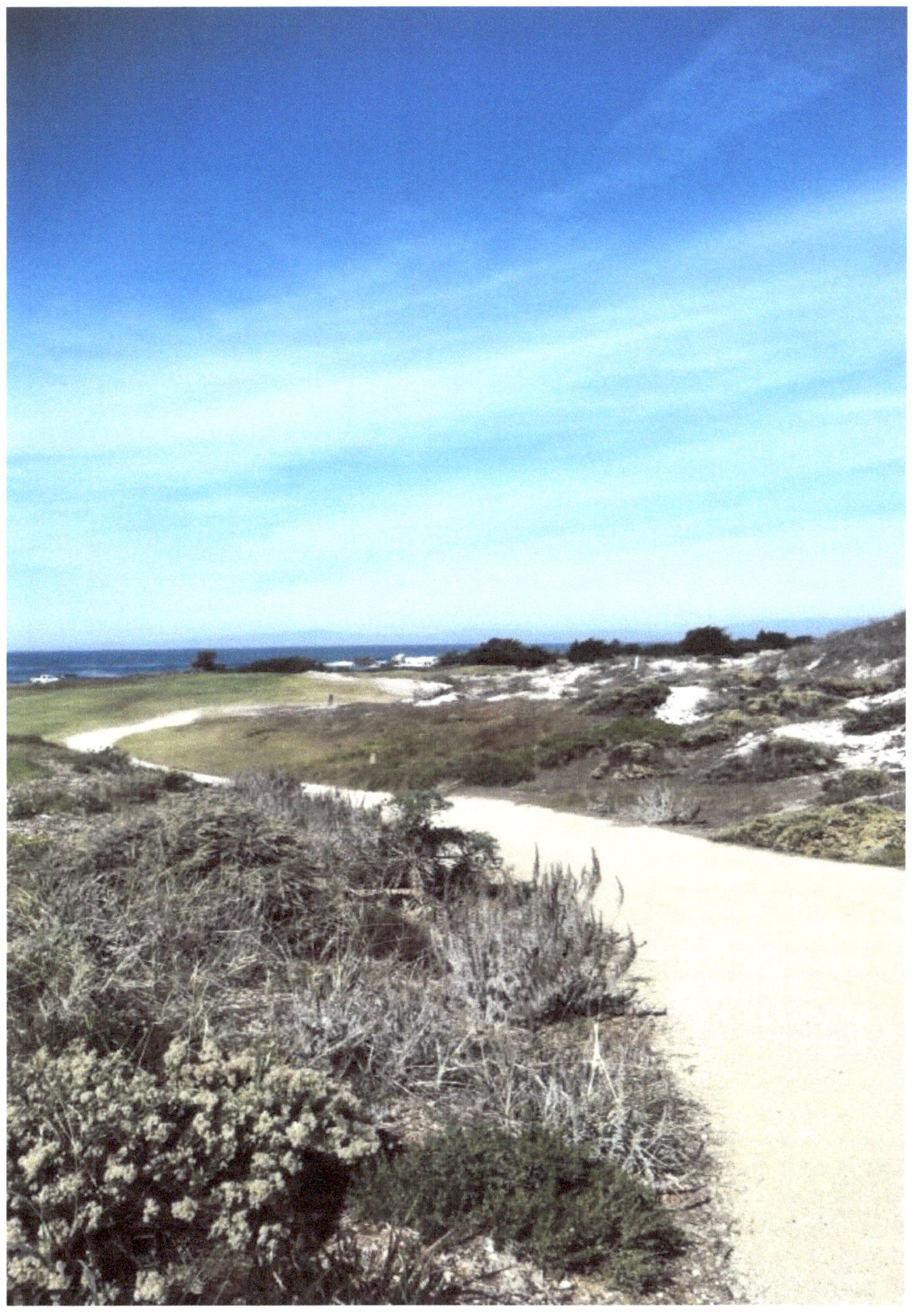

Loneliness

The sun is setting on a nearly perfect day.

I sit, with a glass of red wine in hand

to toast the beautiful sky colors changing.

As this day slips away

I am not sad to see it go.

All of nature's wonder cannot relieve

the hard grasp of loneliness

ever present throughout the day.

Activity pushed it aside for awhile but

like a persistent nagger it reappeared

again and again.

I was reminded that sometimes

even when I am not alone I am lonely.

This is part of the human condition.

I am aware of this and I am also aware

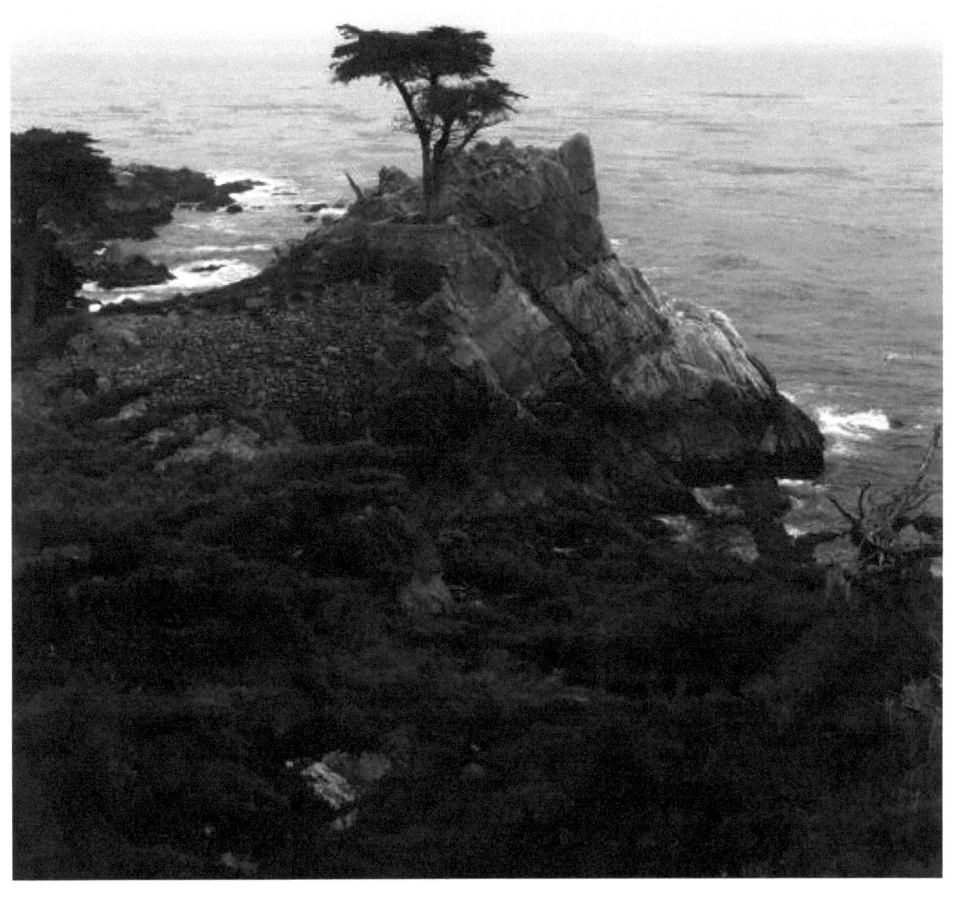

that I cannot cure this alone.

I have resisted close friendships

and falling in love again

after the sting of betrayal left me bitter.

I have been told more than once that we

are each lucky if we have a few

trusted friends in our lifetime,

and especially fortunate if

we have a second chance at love.

I agree.

I want that second chance to love

effortlessly, joyfully, while walking

down a peaceful path that winds slowly

throughout the senior years.

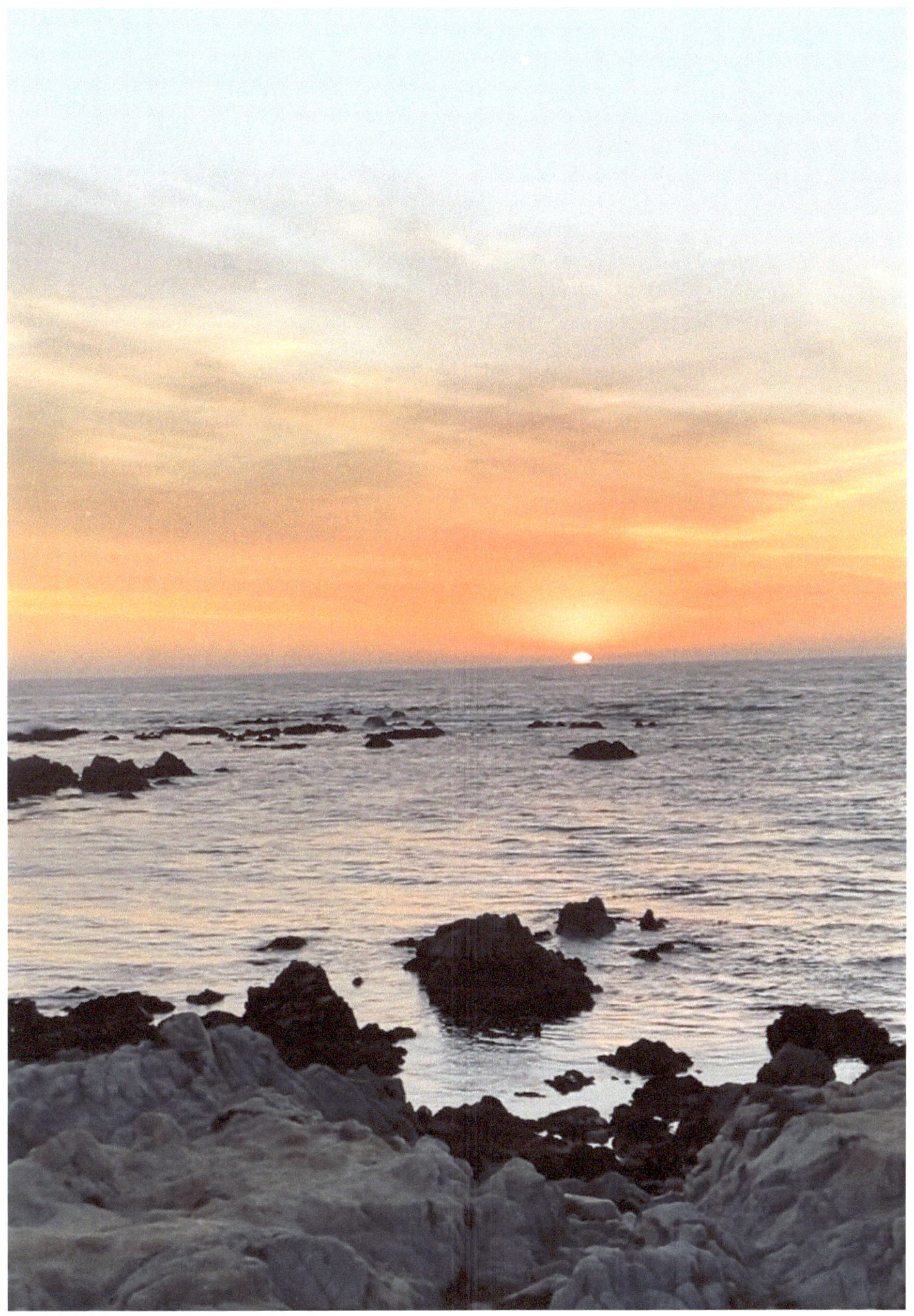

Sisters

Our similarity

goes far beyond the family resemblance.

Our similarity goes far beyond

our jade green eyes.

Our similarity goes far beyond

our telephone voice.

Our similarity goes far beyond

our same sense of humor.

Our similarity goes far beyond

our sometimes brutal honesty.

Our similarity

goes far beyond the secrets

Ewe have kept for each other.

Our similarity goes far beyond

our motherhood experiences.

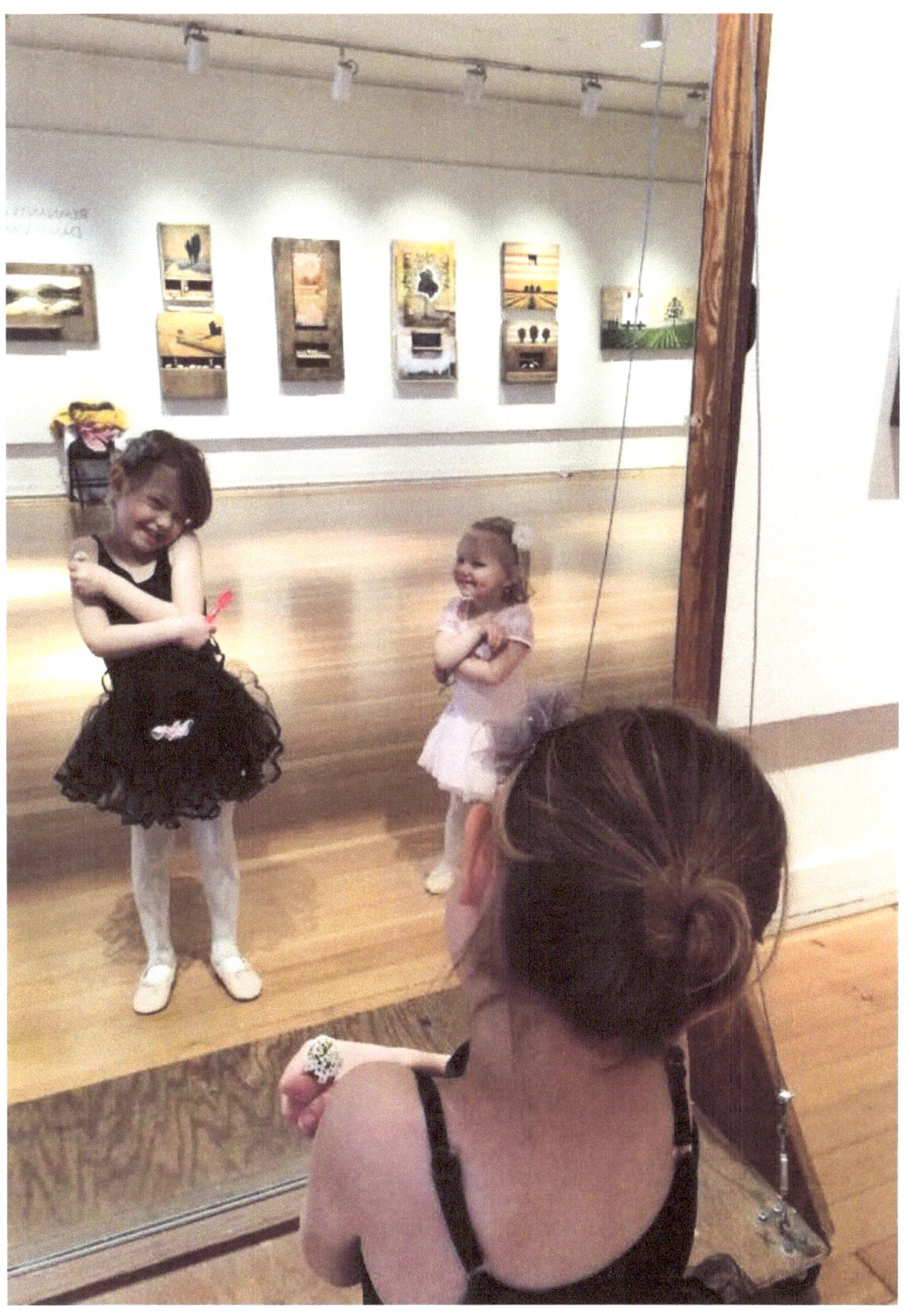

Our similarity goes far beyond

our love of sand, sea, and sunshine.

Our similarity goes far beyond

our support for each other's talents

and the endless encouragement

we provide each other.

Our similarity goes far beyond

the grief we share for the losses

of brothers a Father, friends,

and ex-spouses.

Our similarity goes far beyond

our childhood memories.

Our similarity goes far beyond

our taste in music and

our appreciation of older things.

Our similarity goes far beyond our compassion for others

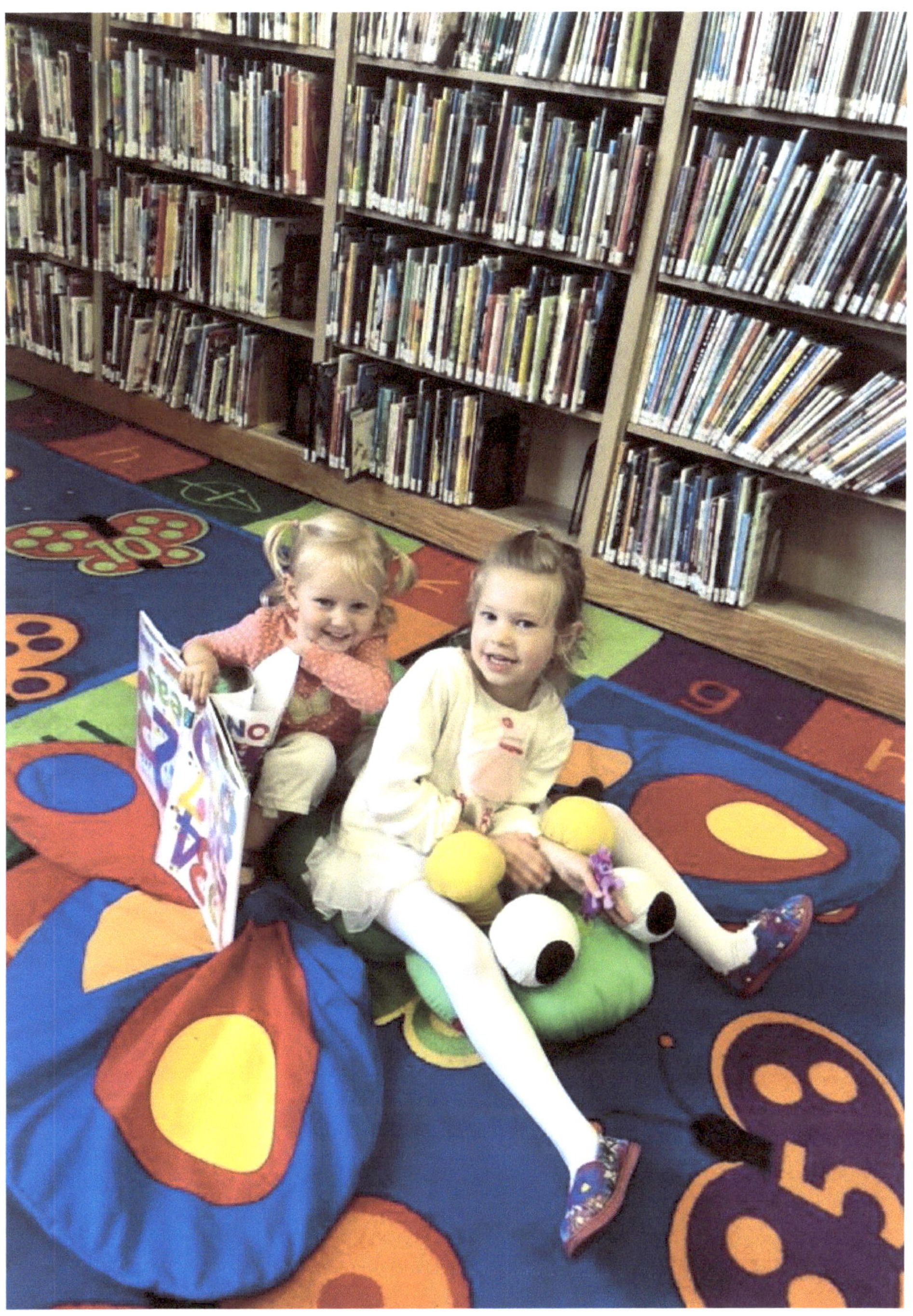

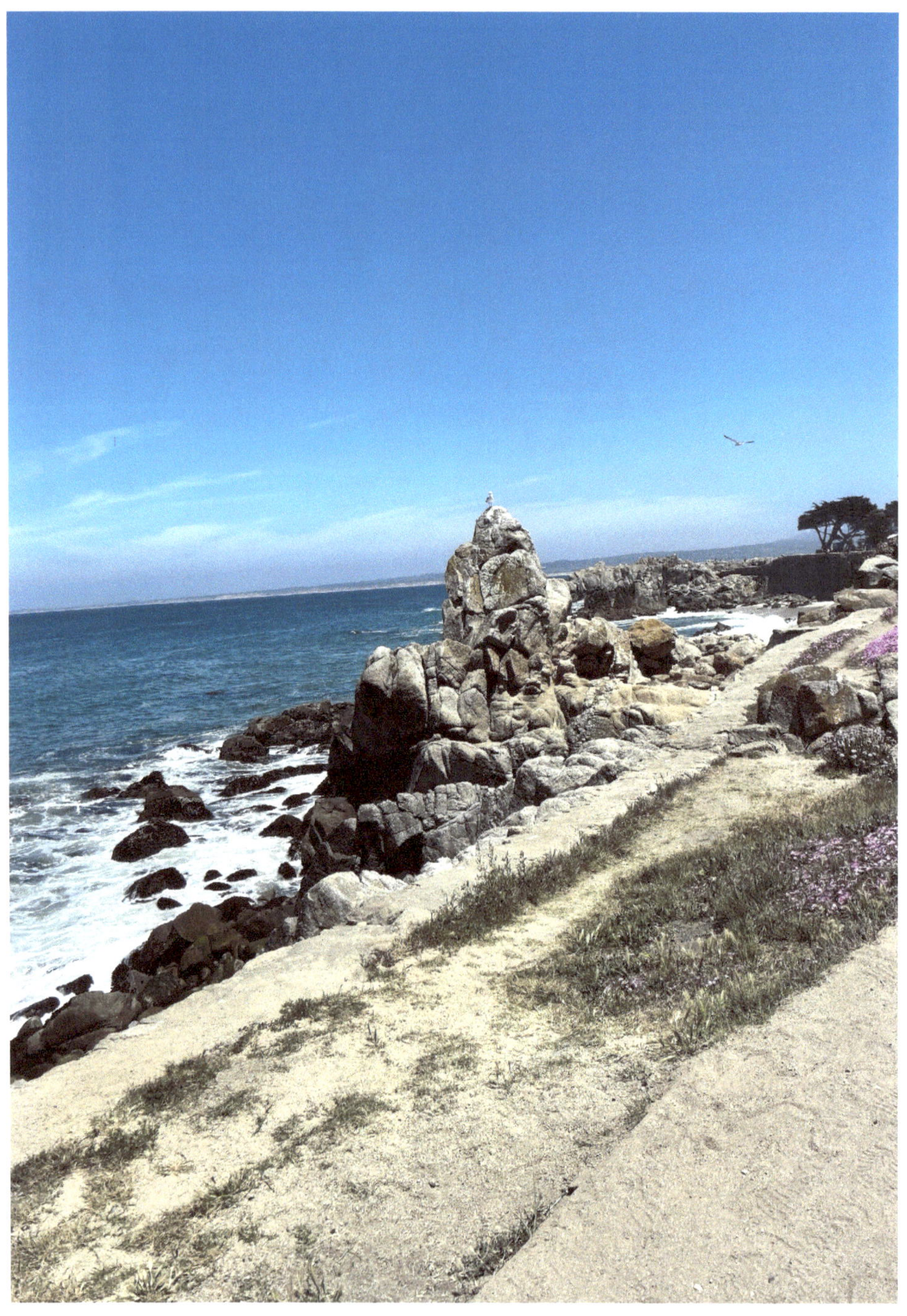

less fortunate and our willingness to help.

Our similarity goes far beyond

the door we leave always open

and the ear to listen always available

and the place we hold forever loving

in the heart that beats strong and steady

for you and me and we two sisters.

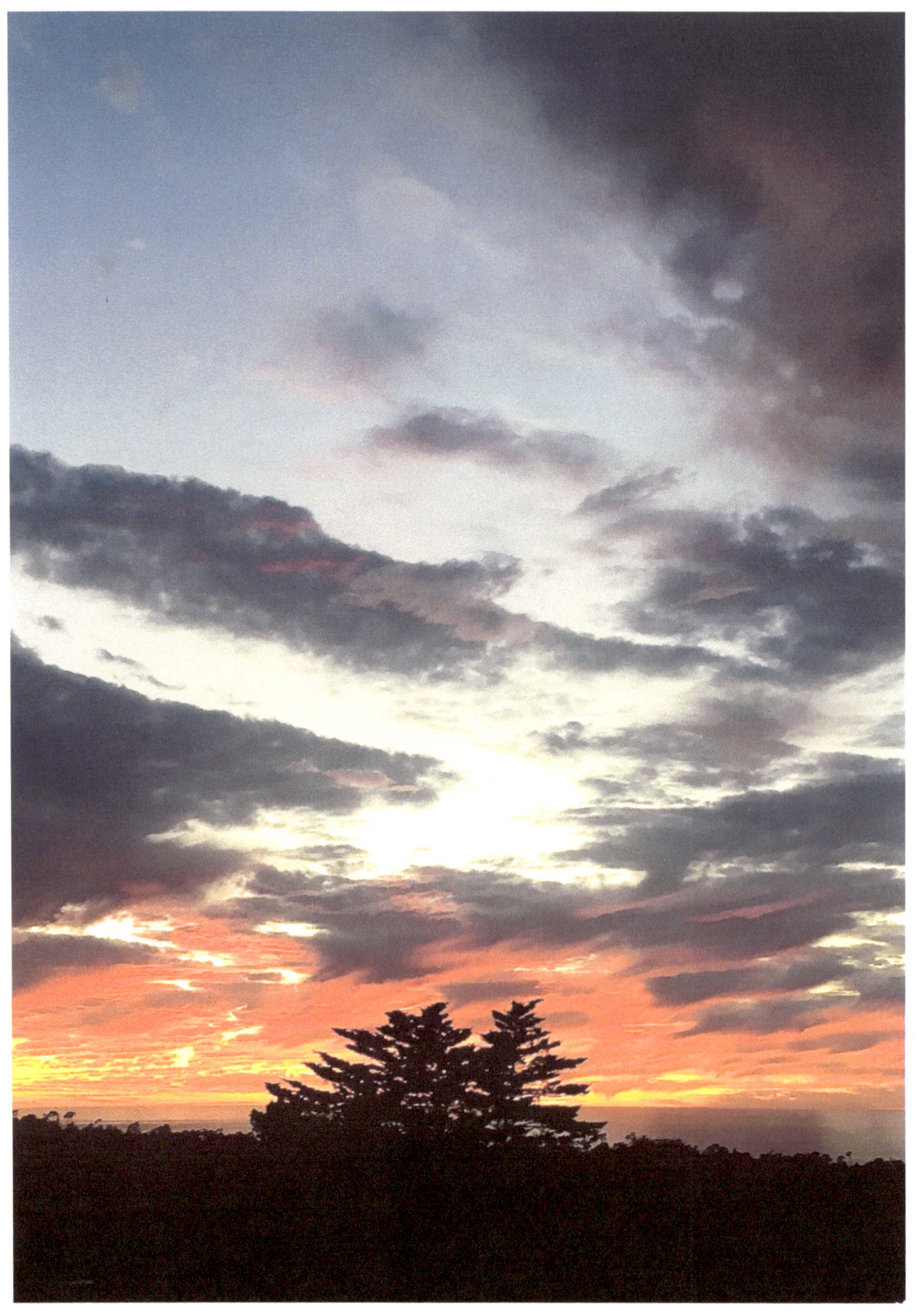

Faith

is an aligned sixth sense that is more real

than what you see or what you hear

or what you smell, or what you taste,

or what you touch.

Profound and yet so simple

to find,

to keep

to hold

to share

to practice living hopeful

to practice inspiring others

to practice being mindful

of one's purpose

and to accept

who you are meant to be

at your place in the universe

where you will journey home

and know it all okay.

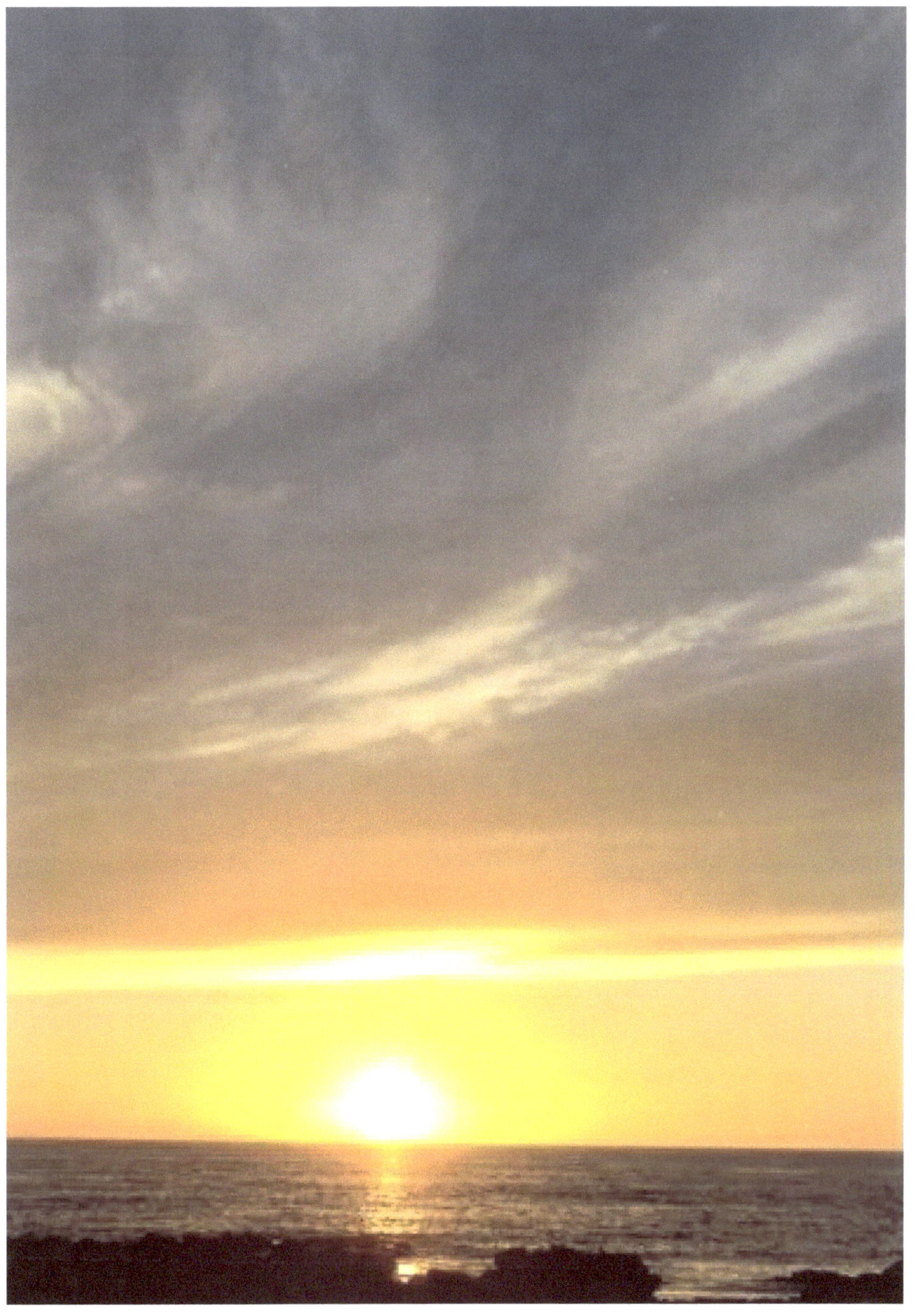

Regret

There it is that ache

that slipped away while sleeping.

This morning's wake wasted no time

in setting back the hands of time

to that moment of regret.

I know it well by now.

I know it grips me still.

I cannot shake the hold it has upon me.

So back in time I go

repeating everything I said,

reliving every word, searching for

some way to change the final blow.

I know it will not work

yet I do it nonetheless.

I just cannot accept that

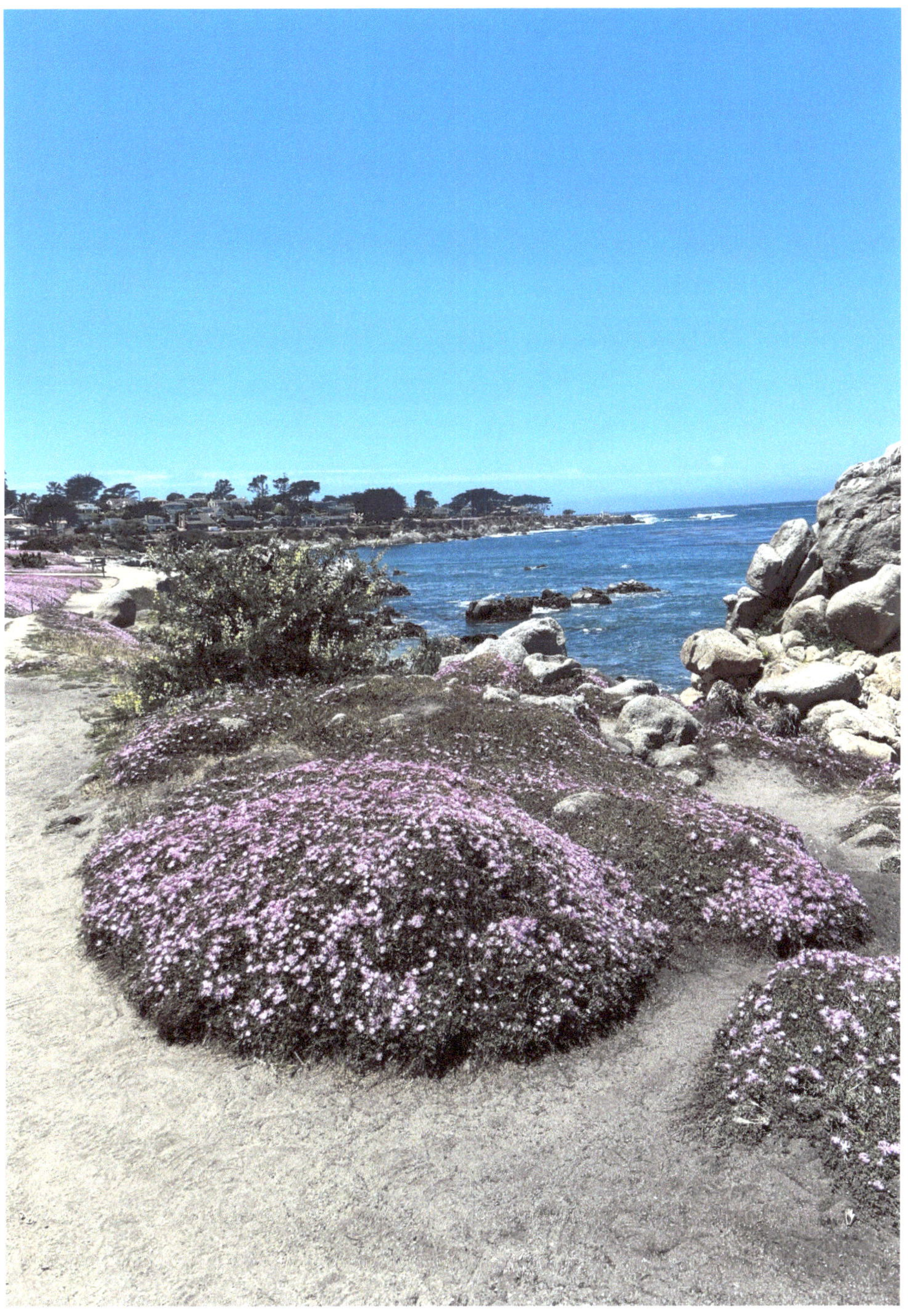

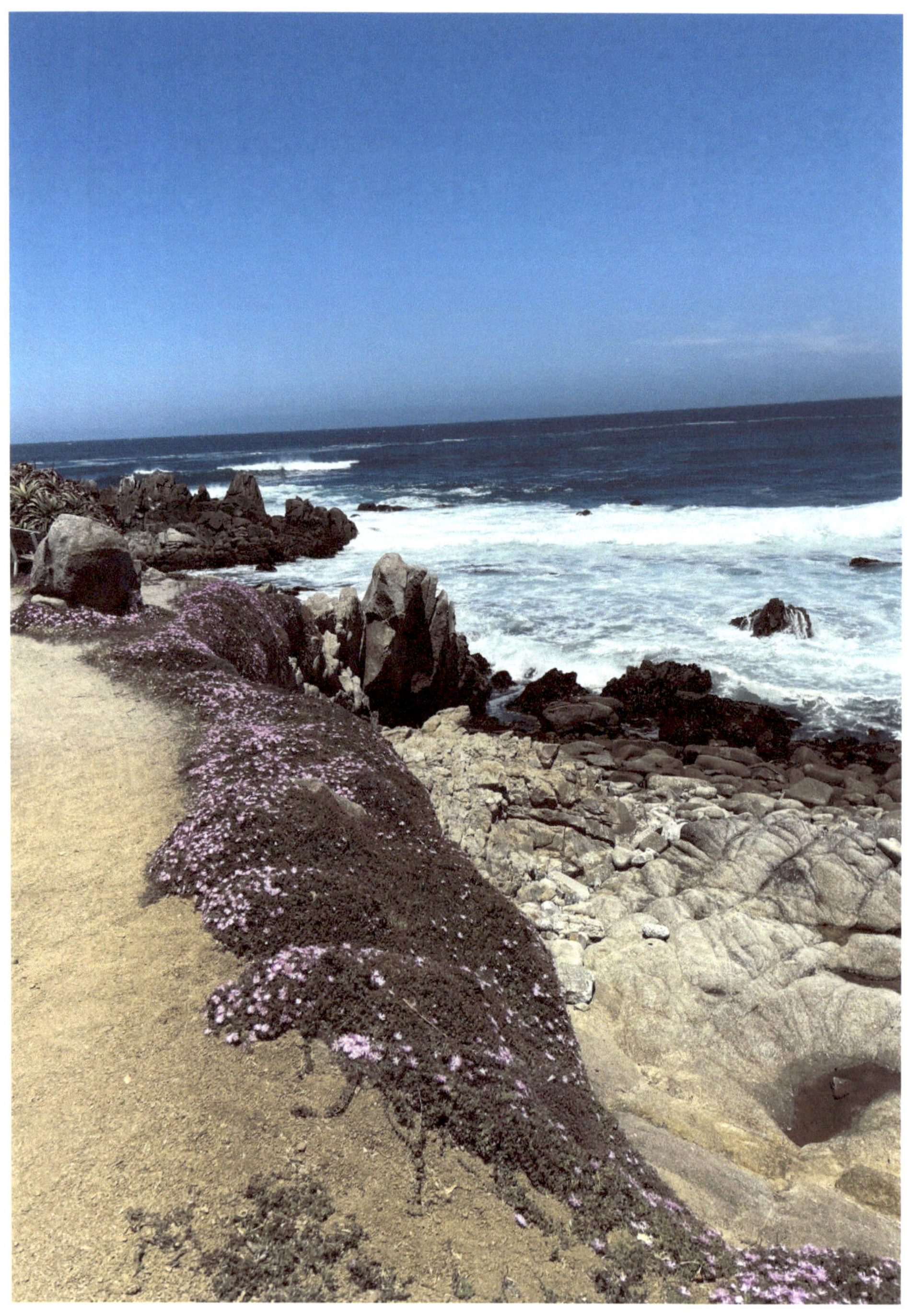

I could be so cruel.

Until I find a way to make up for the hurt

I caused, I'll relive it everyday.

I'll see the slight surprise

flash in your angered eyes.

I'll know I went too far

in all that I had done and said.

I'll watch you walk away

and hear the cracking of your voice

as you say your last goodbye.

This memory will ghost my dreams

I'll stay frozen in regret.

I'll wish I had called you back

so I could explain it all away.

Rearview Mirror

Sometime in some year it started

Maybe when I was quite young

and wanting to see my butterfly wings or

know they were perfect

for a friend to admire.

It doesn't even matter when because

knowing that would not change a thing.

Except maybe knowing would mark

that place in time when I discovered

the importance of the rear view.

From that point in time forward

and for years thereafter,

and even as recently as this morning,

I take part in the same ritual.

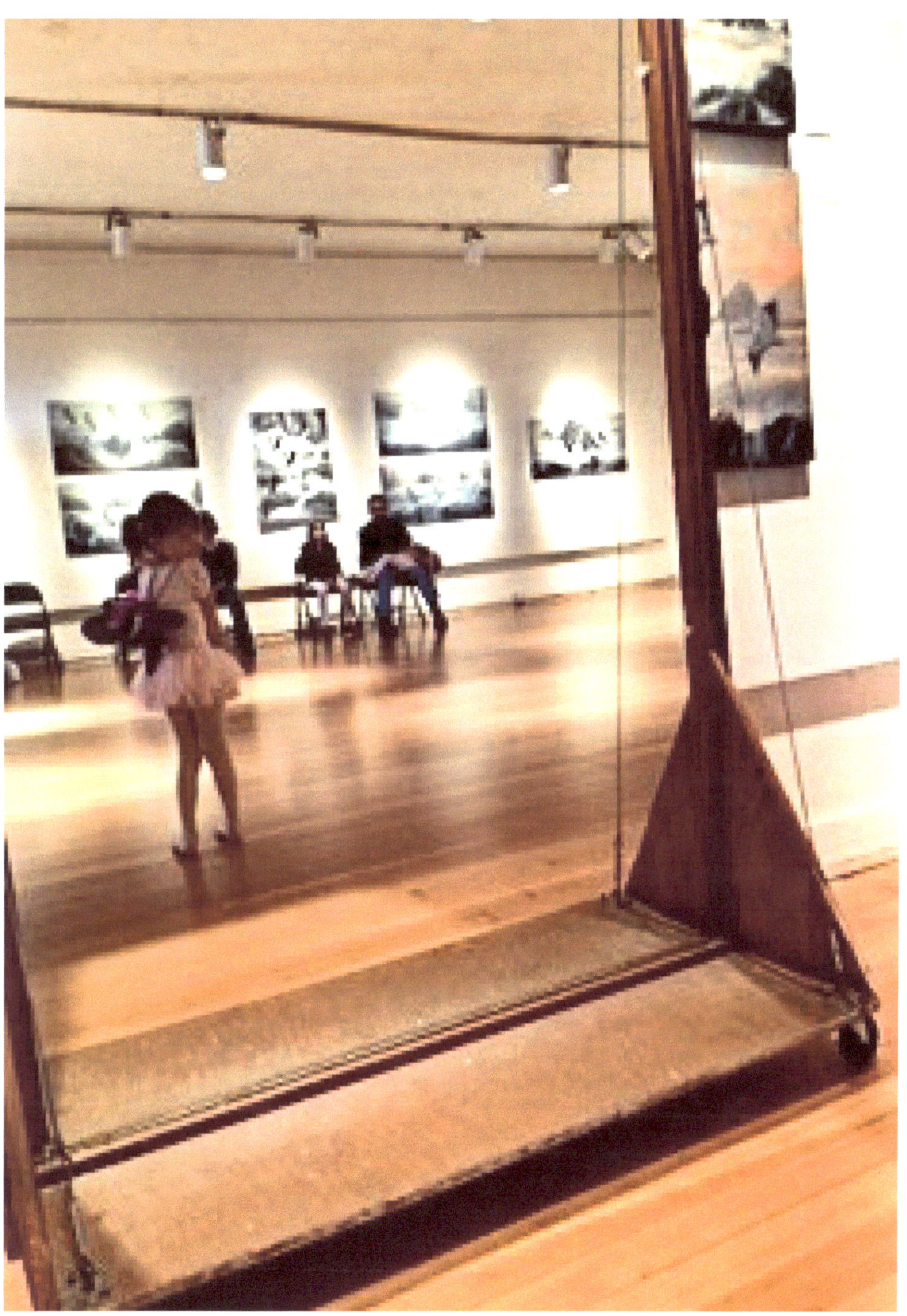

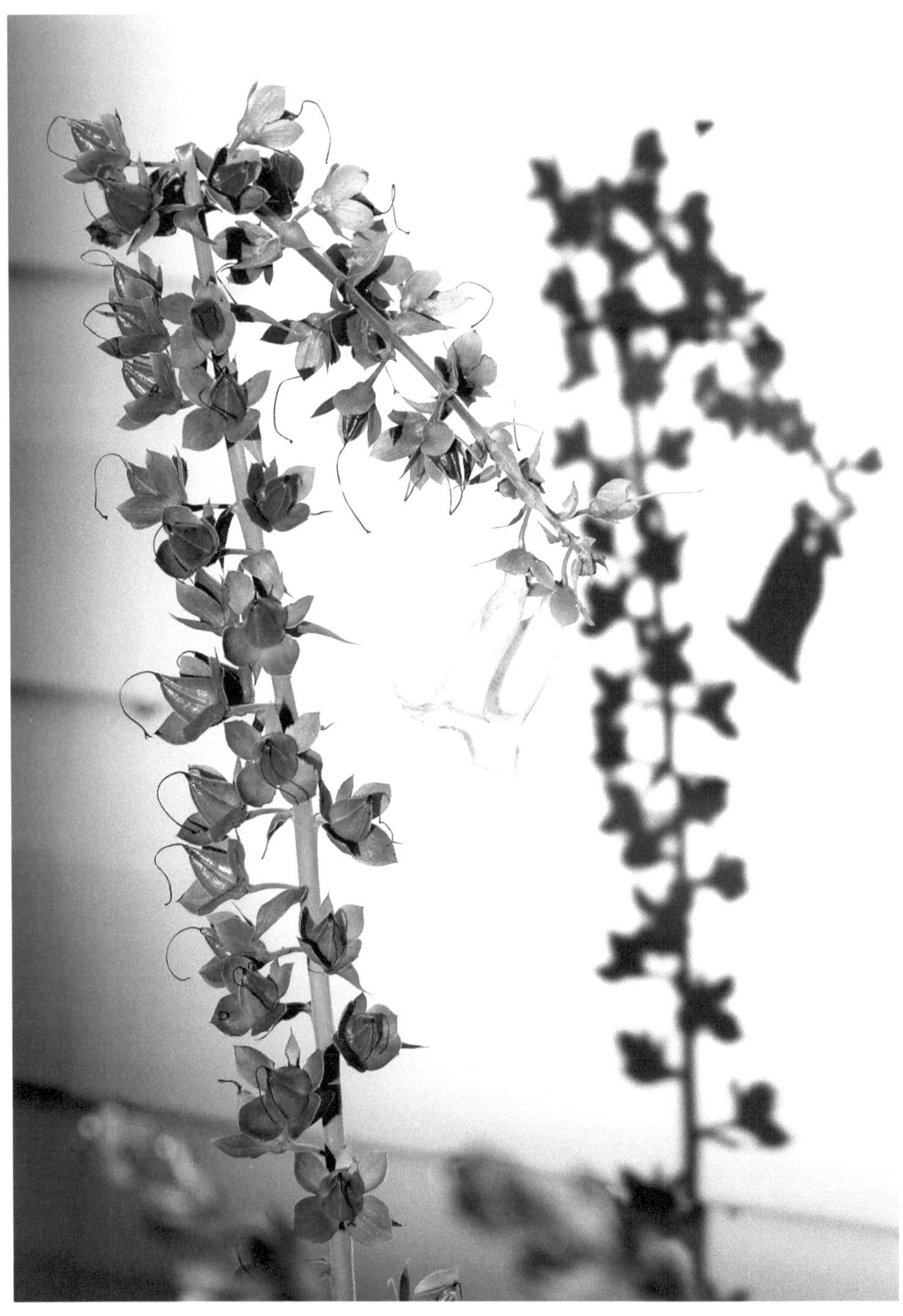

I think most would agree that women
of every color gracing space throughout
the world find themselves completing
their daily dress routine by stealing a
quick glance of the rear view mirrored.

Dream Weaver

Oh to make peace

with an unintended fate as this.

This end of a road so long

with so many turns

and most of them difficult to navigate.

This end to a dream at first filled

with so much promise.

Until there was you and your desire

to control the unfolding of my dream.

You with all your ideas but without a plan.

No!

Do not steal away this dream of mine!

You who are not me.

You who have not suffered.

You who have not been alone

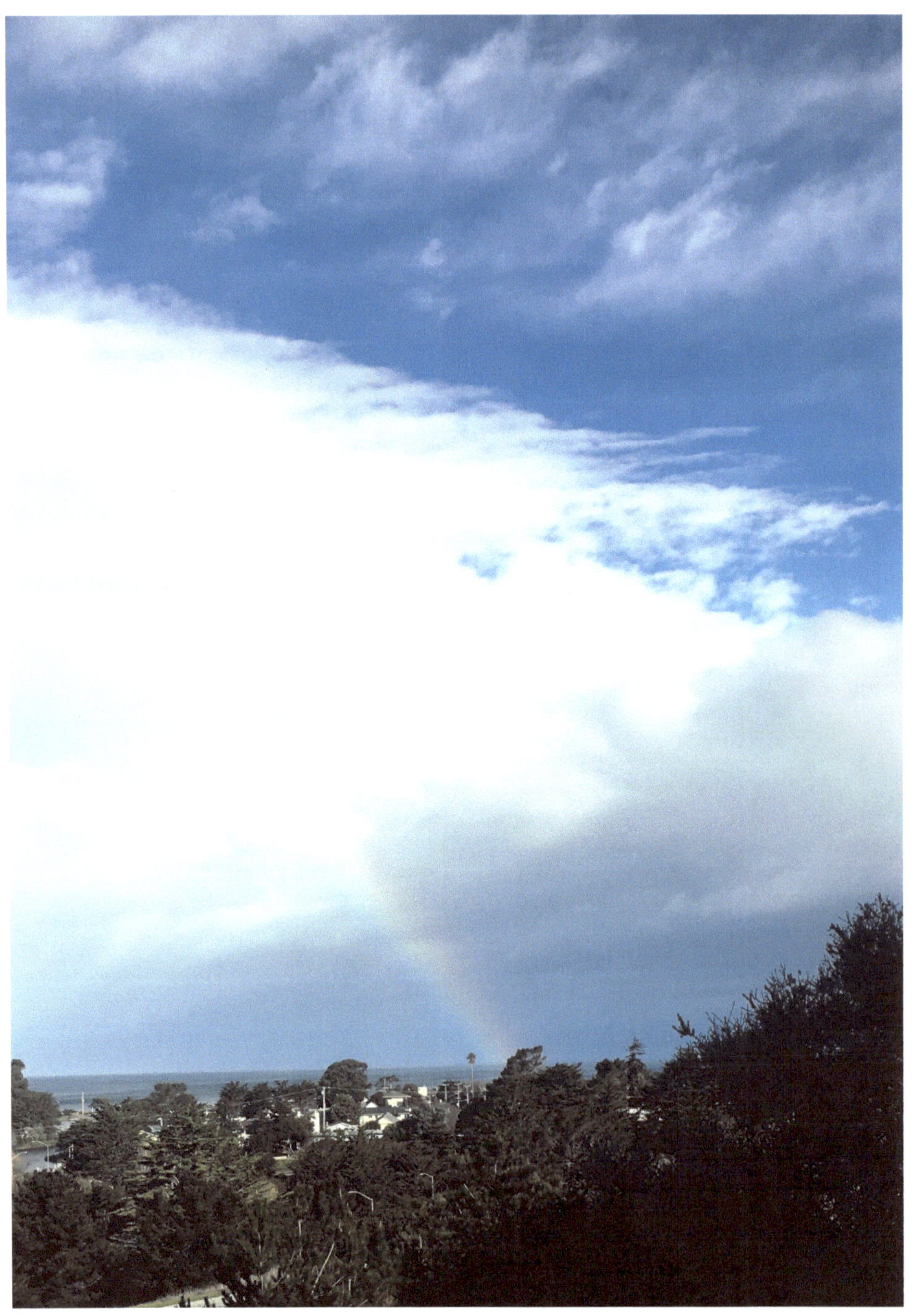

all these years.

You who have not had to listen

to the unkind words in silence.

You who have not been victim

to those many nasty deeds.

You who think you know me.

You who think yourself noble

You who think you should edit my world

by destroying my dream.

A dream that has shifted through time.

A dream reshaped by occurrences

out of my control.

A dream shattered once again

but with a part kept alive still

through a light reflecting

from the broken edges.

A light bright enough to inspire hope.

A light infused with

the color of imagination.

A light that shines upon the thoughts

that move me forward. A light just ahead

of my path into the future where I will

mourn away this last dream

and open my heart to the next.

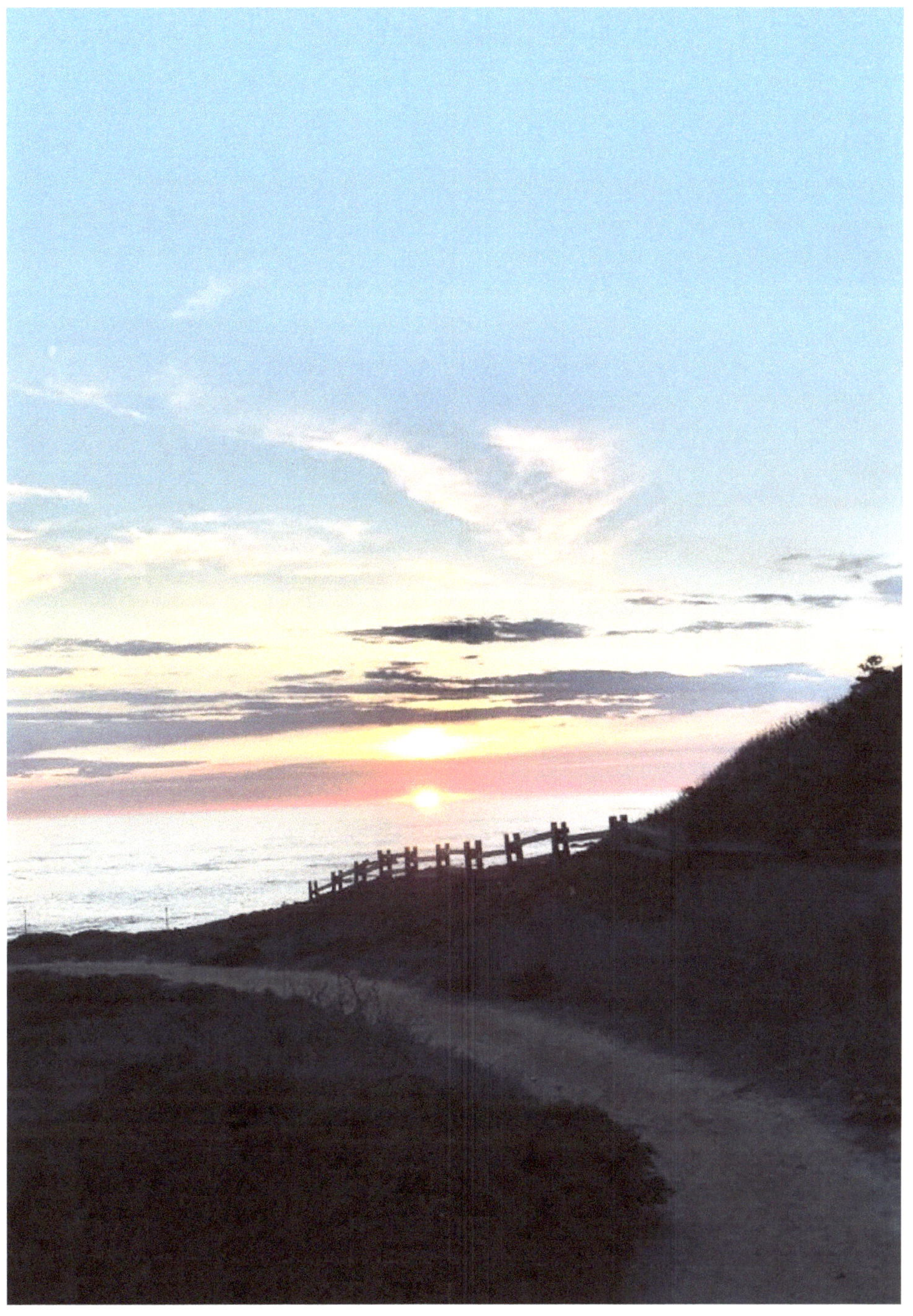

If I Had a Tattoo

If I had a tattoo it must be of such
significance that it could replace the scar
left behind from my first set of stitches
required after I fell face first into
the corner of the metal milk box
sitting outside the front door
of my childhood home.
Or the small scars on my right knee
still transparent enough after all
these years to show the cinders beneath
left behind after dragging Stevens Lane
when I tipped the mini-bike and refused
to let go. Or the two finger knuckle scar
caused by boiling sugar that spilled over
the stovetop when little brother

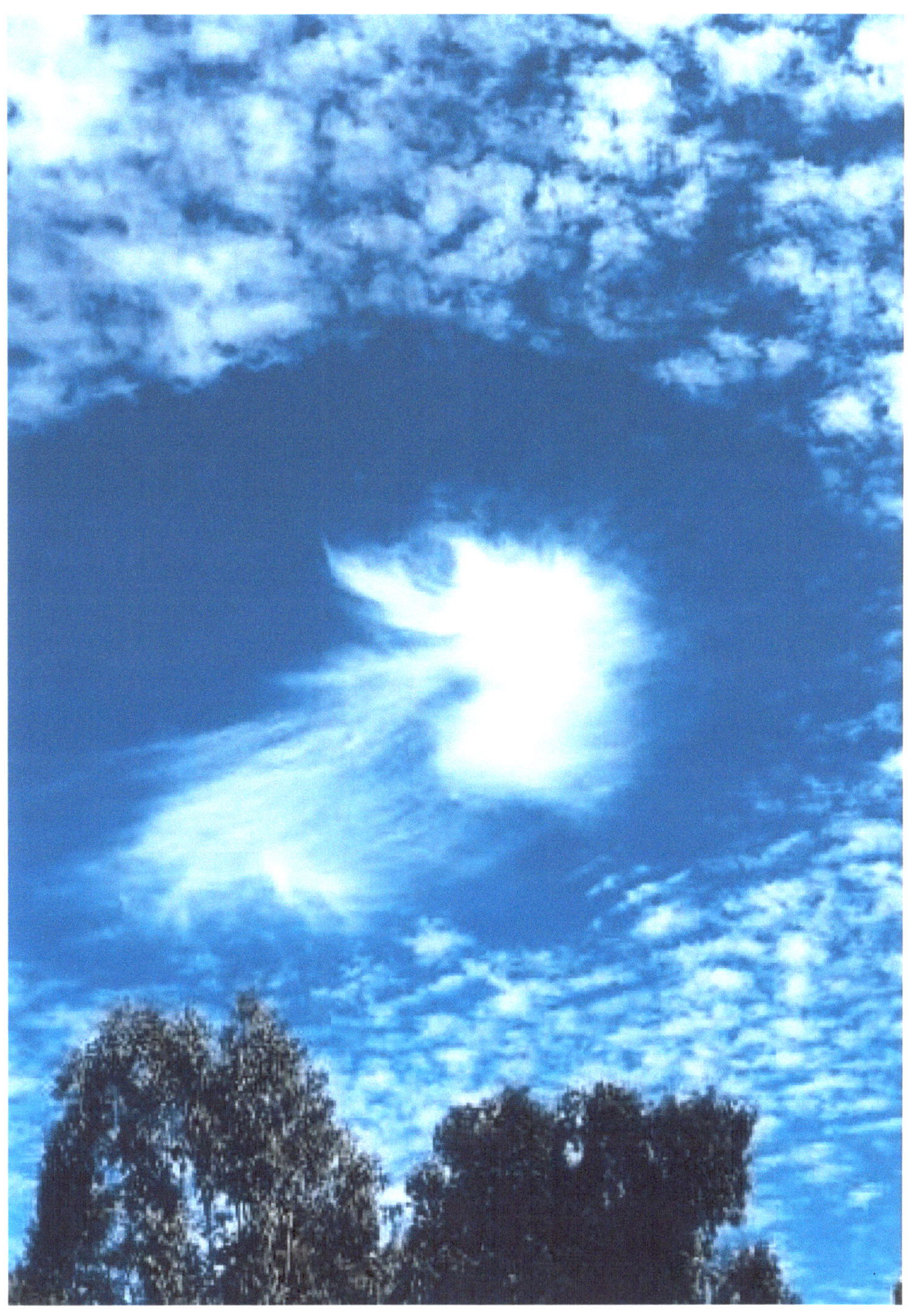

pulled on the pan handle for a look.
Or the surgical scars left behind
from removing freckles and moles
and what sometimes grew beneath.
Yes, I may look more serious with the
scar between my eyes;
Yes, I am still proud of those cinders.
Yes, I turn pan handles inward.
Yes, I do watch for changes on my skin.
Until there comes a day when I can
replace all or any of my scars and all or
any of the memories they have the power
to recall, with one tatoo or more,
I cannot see the point.

This Place

I am familiar with this place.

I have many times walked

the whole of the town.

I have sat among the other locals

to eat and to pray.

I have danced behind

the tail of the dragon at Chautauqua Hall

and have been held captured by the

princess' tale while I watched the dragon

breathe fire over the bay.

I have been enchanted by

the historic adobes and I have walked

the path of history.

A history that includes stories

of local ghost sightings.

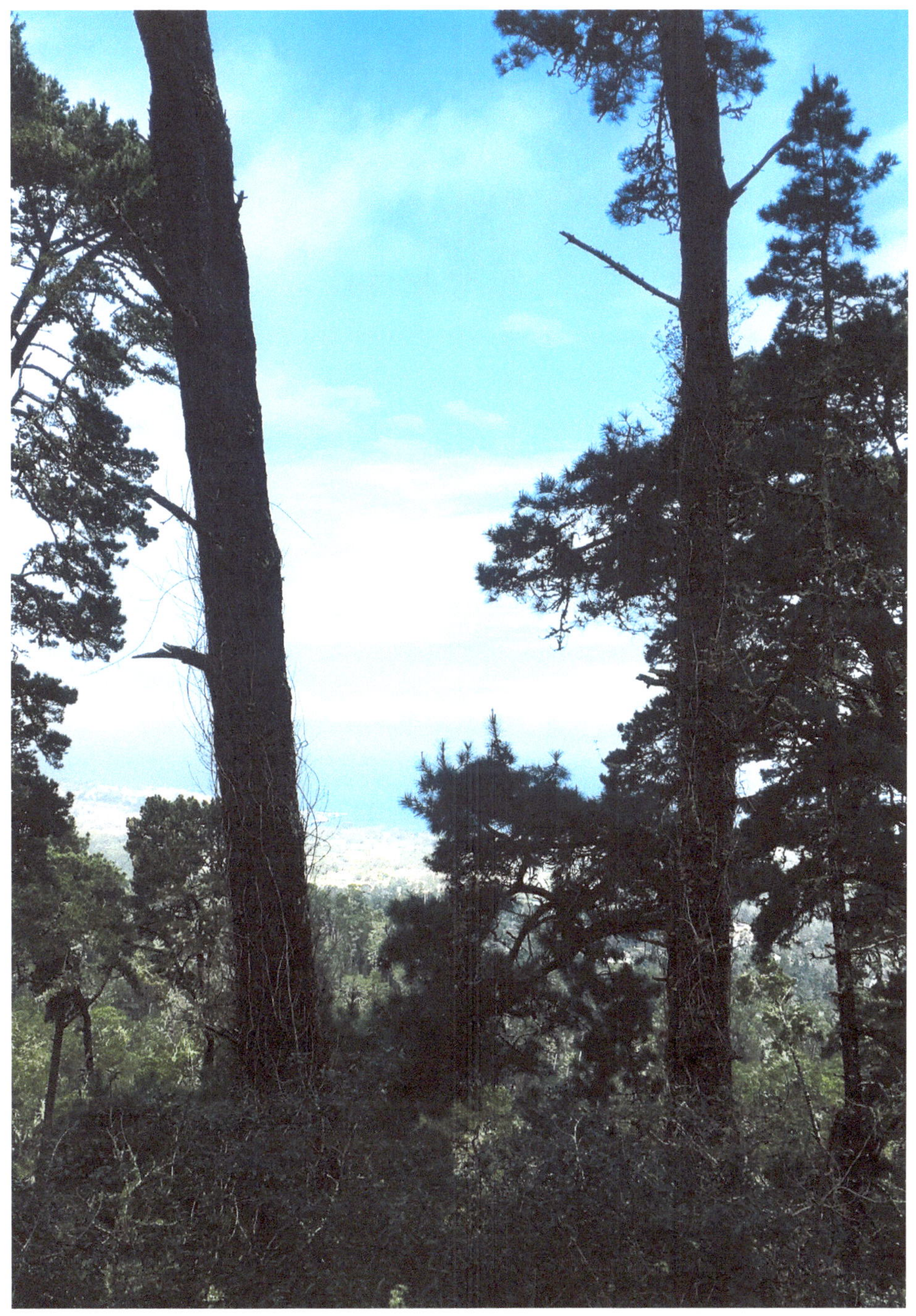

Sightings of a young boy

in early 20th century clothing

playing in a rear yard, or of a glimpse

of pirates darting behind Cypress.

The experience may be audible,

like hearing the midday clip-clop of

a horse trotting down a cobblestone street

abutting the Cooper Molera Adobe.

This place is where John Steinbeck

put stick to paper finishing the pages

of Cannery Row. While this aspiring

writer wondered the rooms of his house

she imagined what he might say if he

found her among his furnishings and

personal belongings.

"So you think yourself a writer?

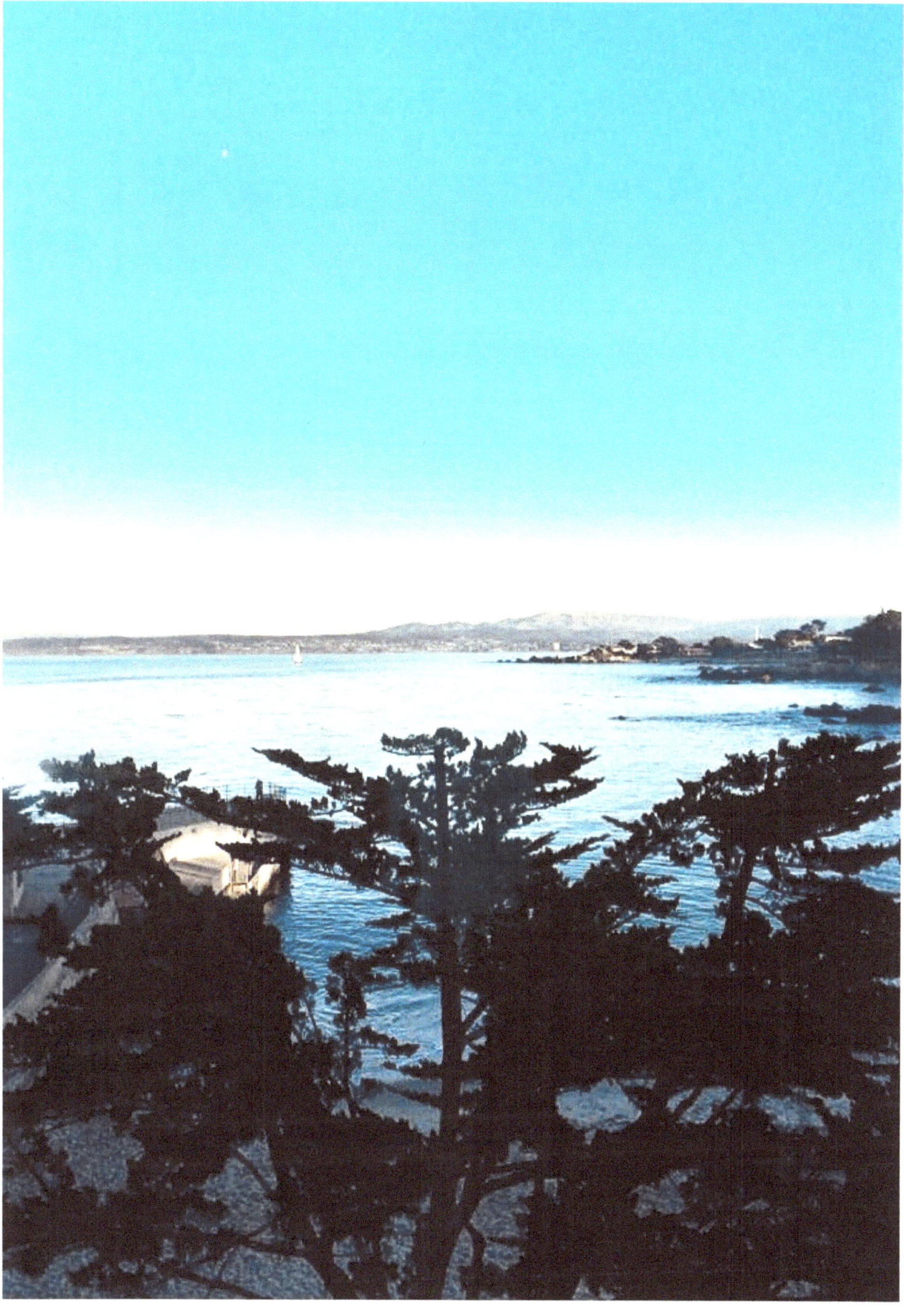

"Get on with it then!"

Remnants of the past are found

in Steinbeck's books,

in the cornerstones of buildings

left untouched, and in

the traditions that weave throughout

the social fabric of this place.

Throughout events repeated each year.

In a climate where even

on the brightest of days

the fog may roll in thick opposite the

sunset, engulfing everything in its mist.

Looking like smoke, but unlike that

choking burn fog brings a cool

sense of clarity, like a weather front

moving in to sweep out and replace

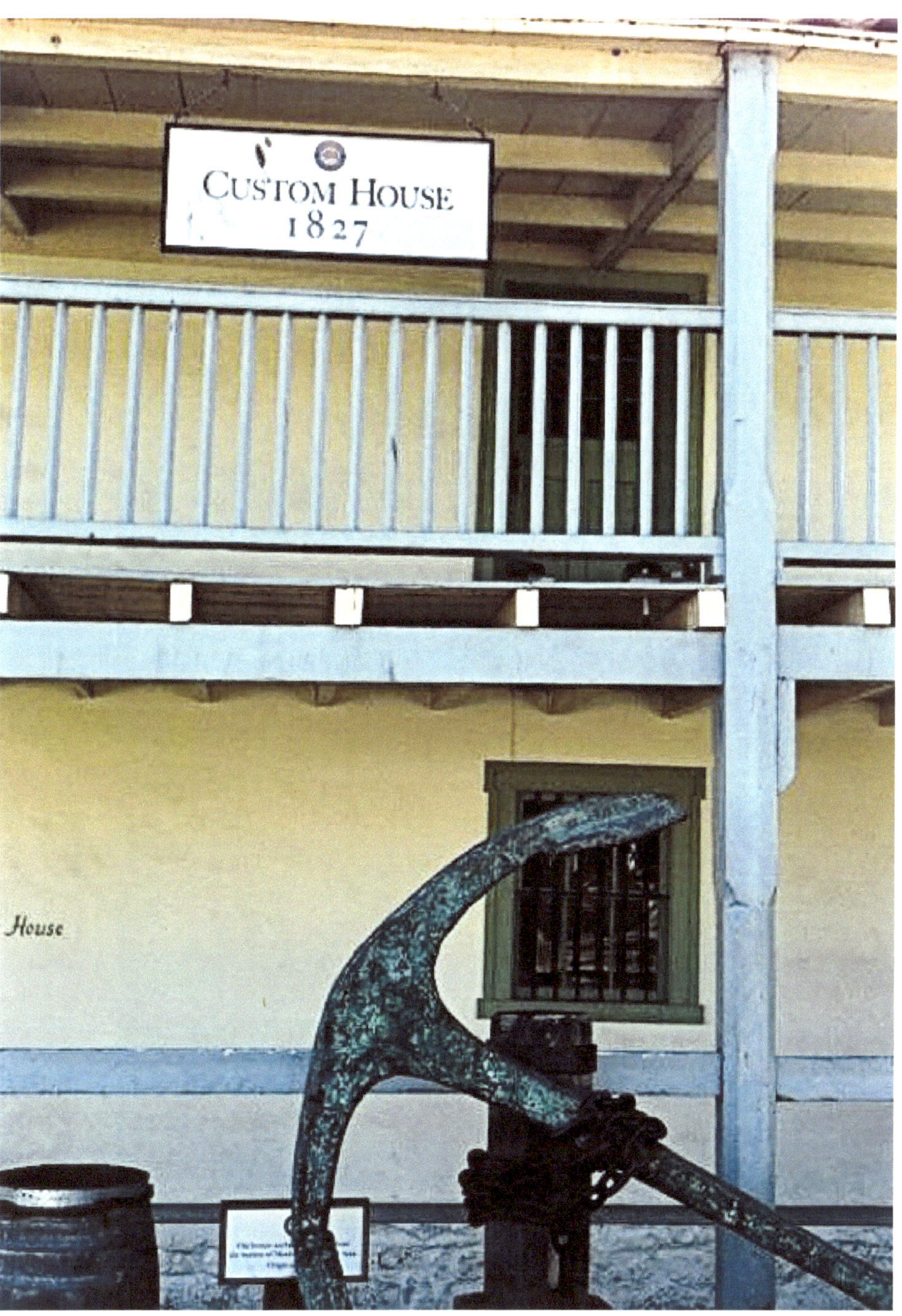
CUSTOM HOUSE
1827
House

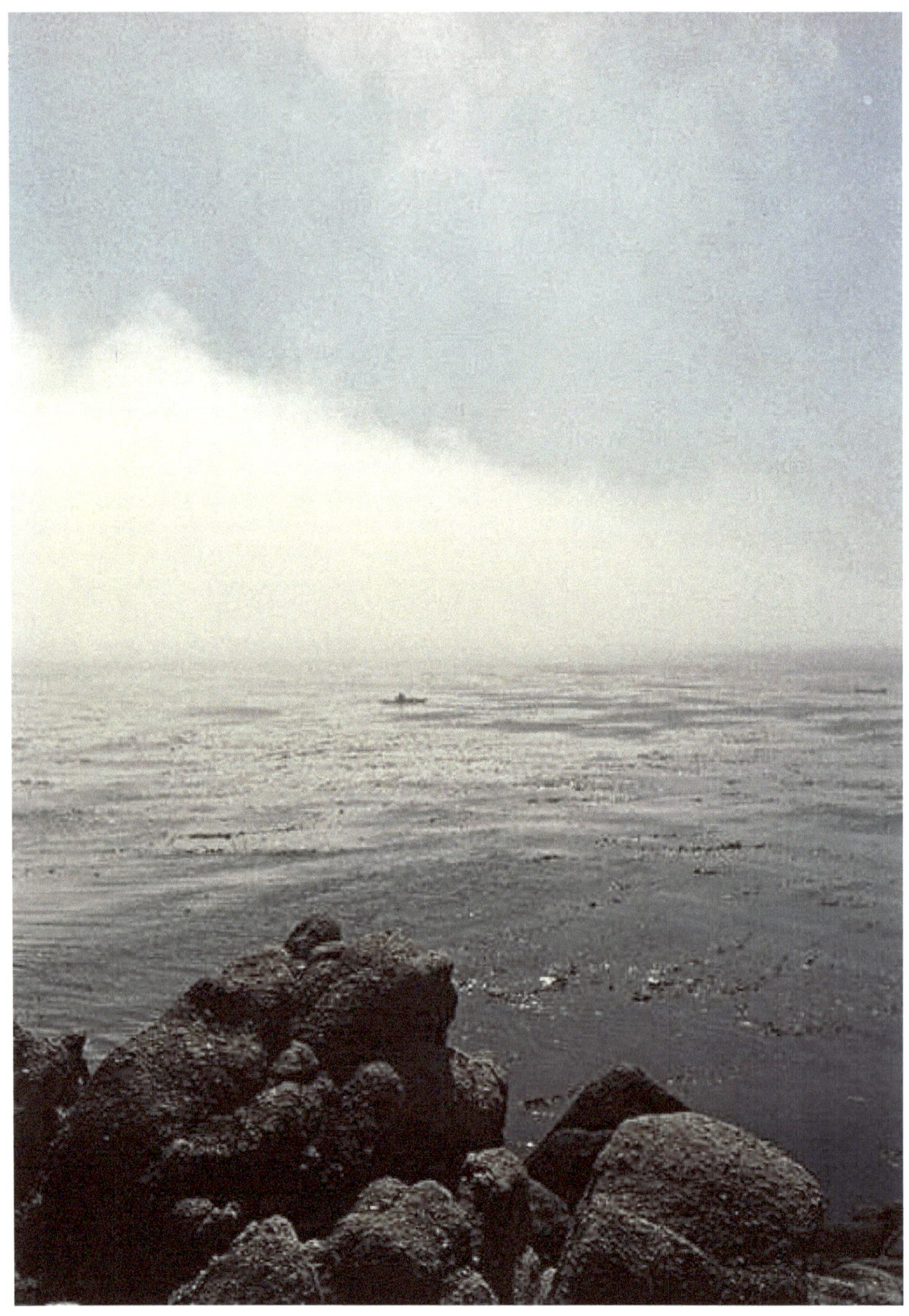

the stagnant air.

Replace

all

but

the historical beauty of this place.

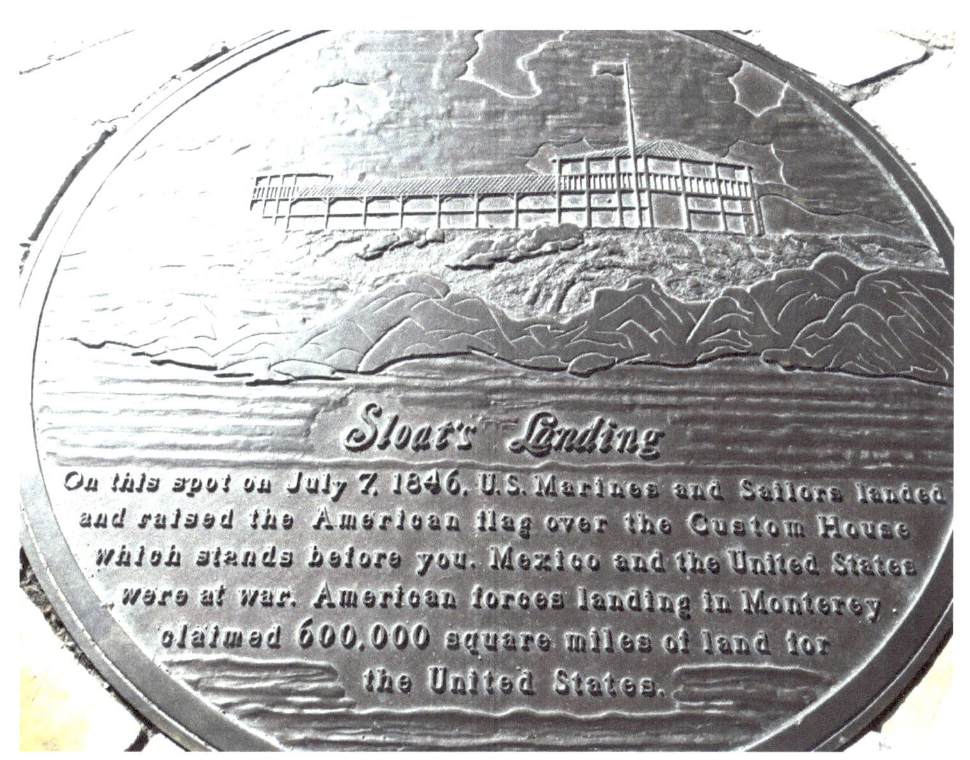

Mending Fences

We each have our limits

for things like what we choose to tolerate

in the behavior of others,

especially when the behavior

has the potential to trigger

a negative emotional response.

Once the threshold of intolerance

is crossed there is no reversal.

The relationship is now changed.

The change happened instantly

when the mind realized

the power of that interaction.

Power to trigger the emotion we had

no intention to release into that moment.

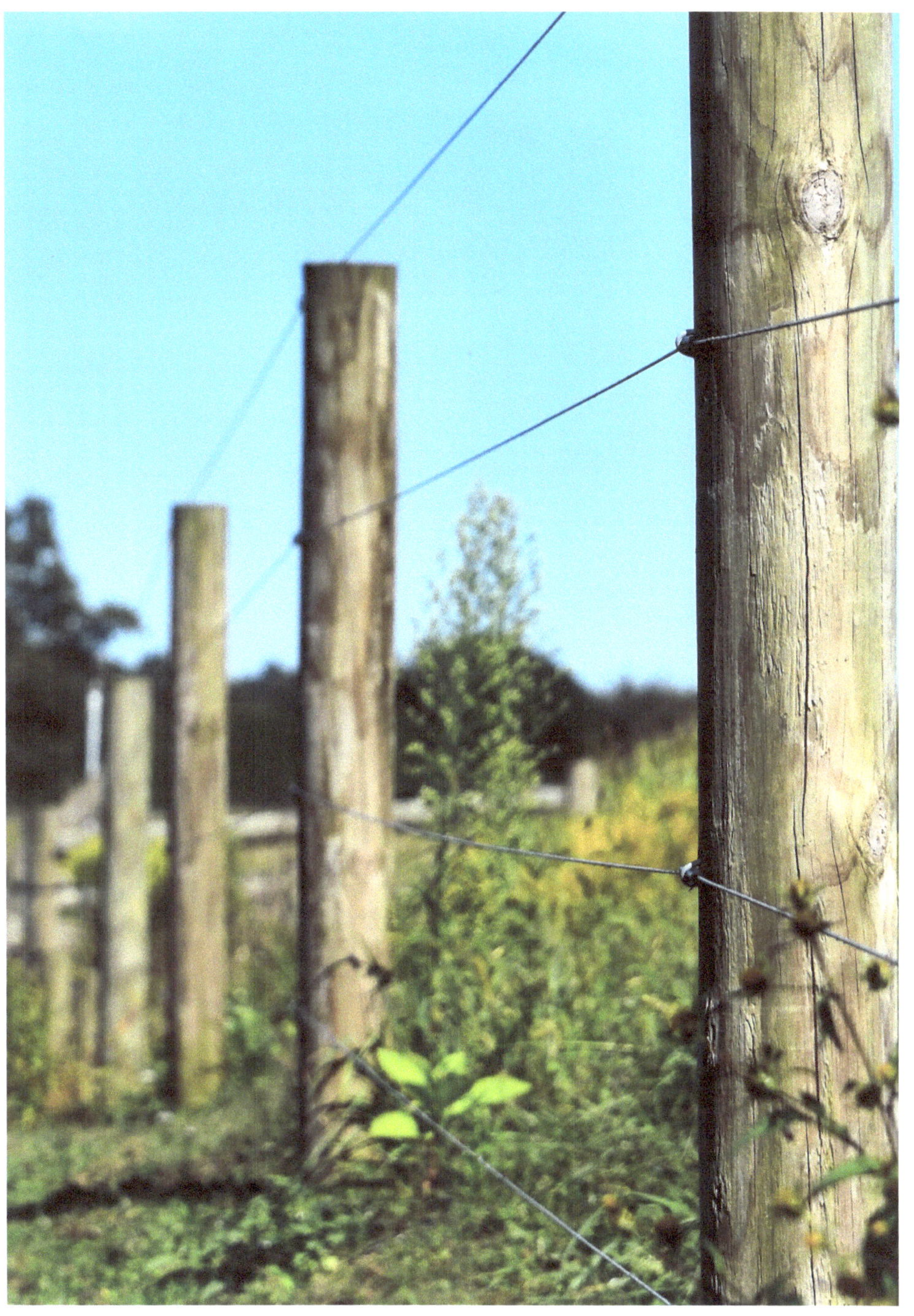

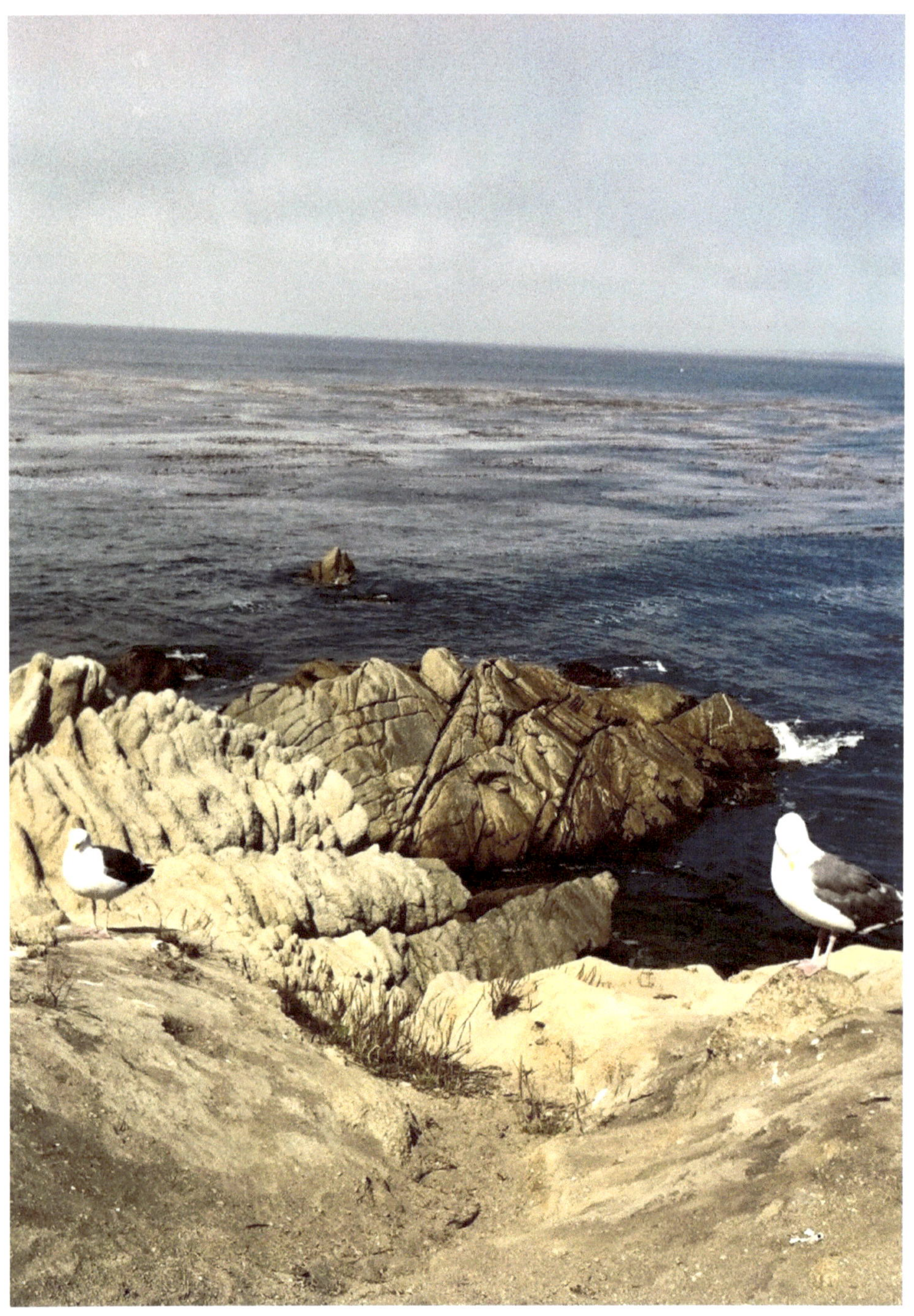

But released it is, even if in thought alone.
A controlled release, where we pretend
that we have no care, where we pretend
not to notice, pretend we are not hurt
by the words said or the deed done.
We each have our triggers spawned
by hurtful experiences.
There was a first to start it off,
then came another, and another, and so it
goes for years. A groove is worn in our
emotional response pathway that
although at first unpleasant grows
comfortable, familiar. Each new
occurrence wears the groove deeper until
we come to expect conflict.
We allow our automated response to steal

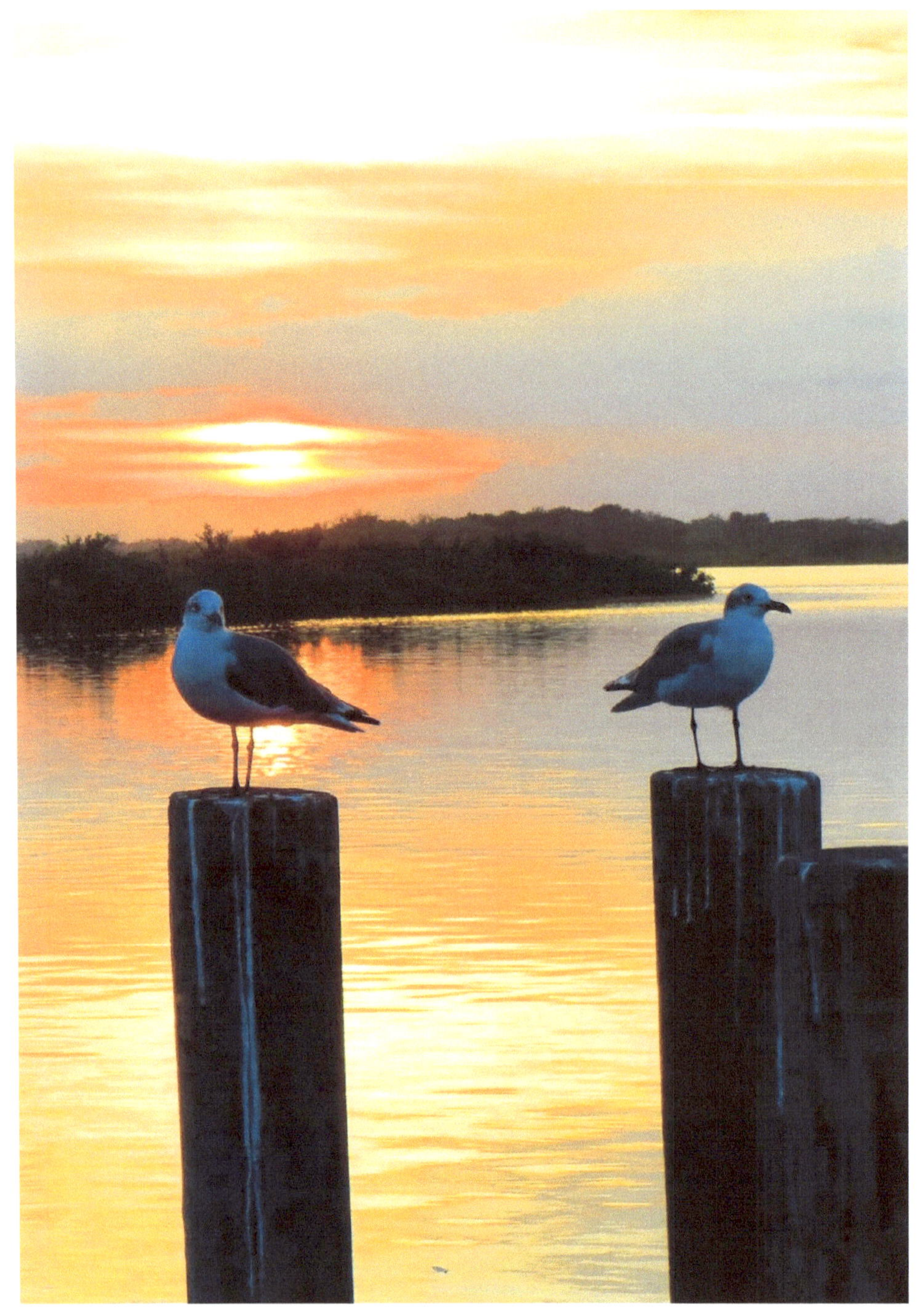

the choice we have in how we react.

If we can stop ourselves in this moment,

realize we can choose our response we

can regain control over our emotion.

While engaged in confrontation, if efforts

are not made at mending in an attempt to

restore the status quo, our mind may

never think it worthy, instead sinking it

to a subprime level, a waste of our time.

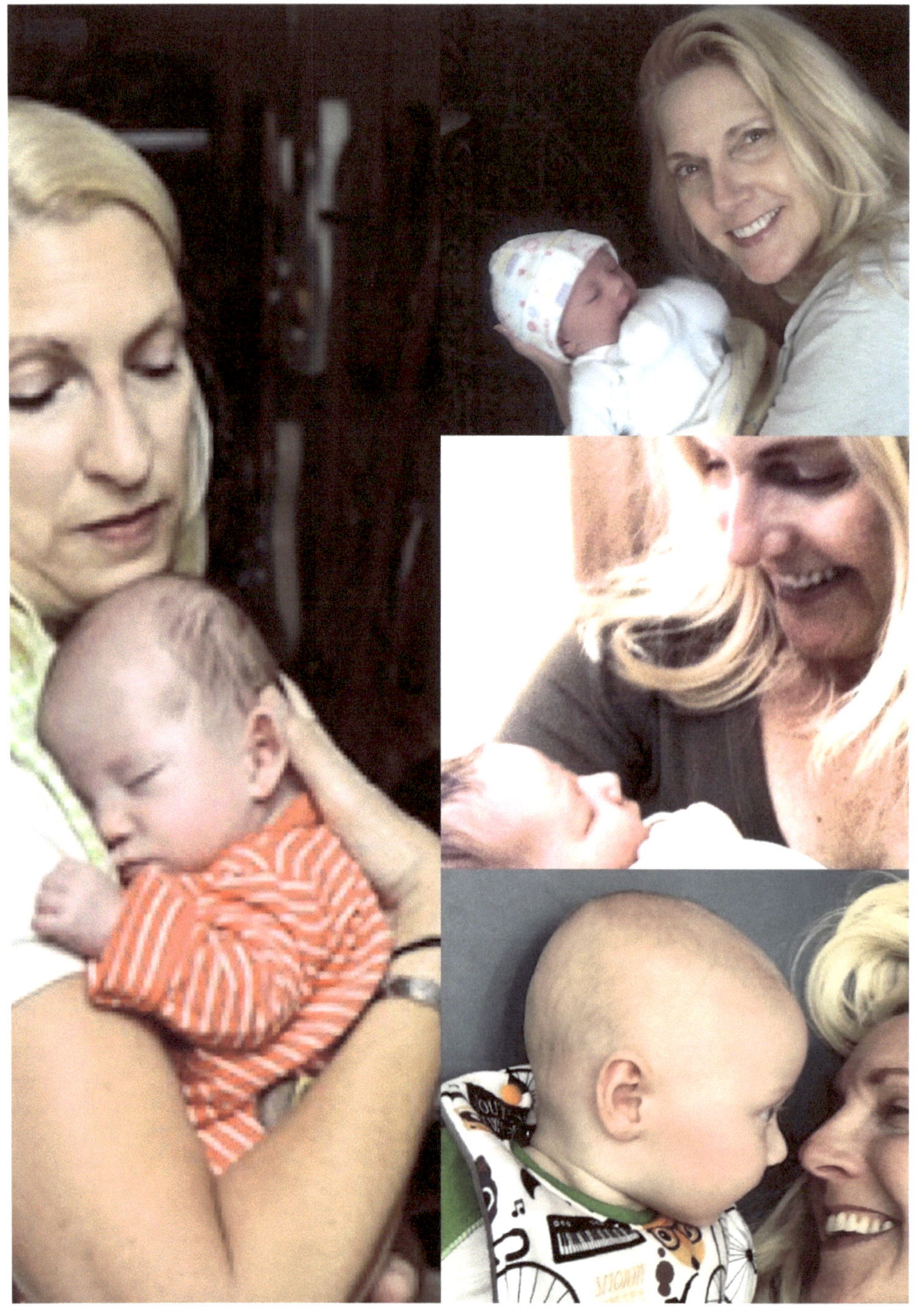

Grandma

The sweetest reward is mine today.

I swell with joyful bliss.

This is the day that you are born

and I am forever changed.

It is not for pride, or for relief

of knowing you are well.

It is for a new purpose, unspoken,

a gift to me understood.

With that in mind I make this oath

to each of you my love

No matter what may be for you

as you grow your way along,

I'll sit or walk or stand with you

and you will keep me strong.

I'll see through your eyes the wonder

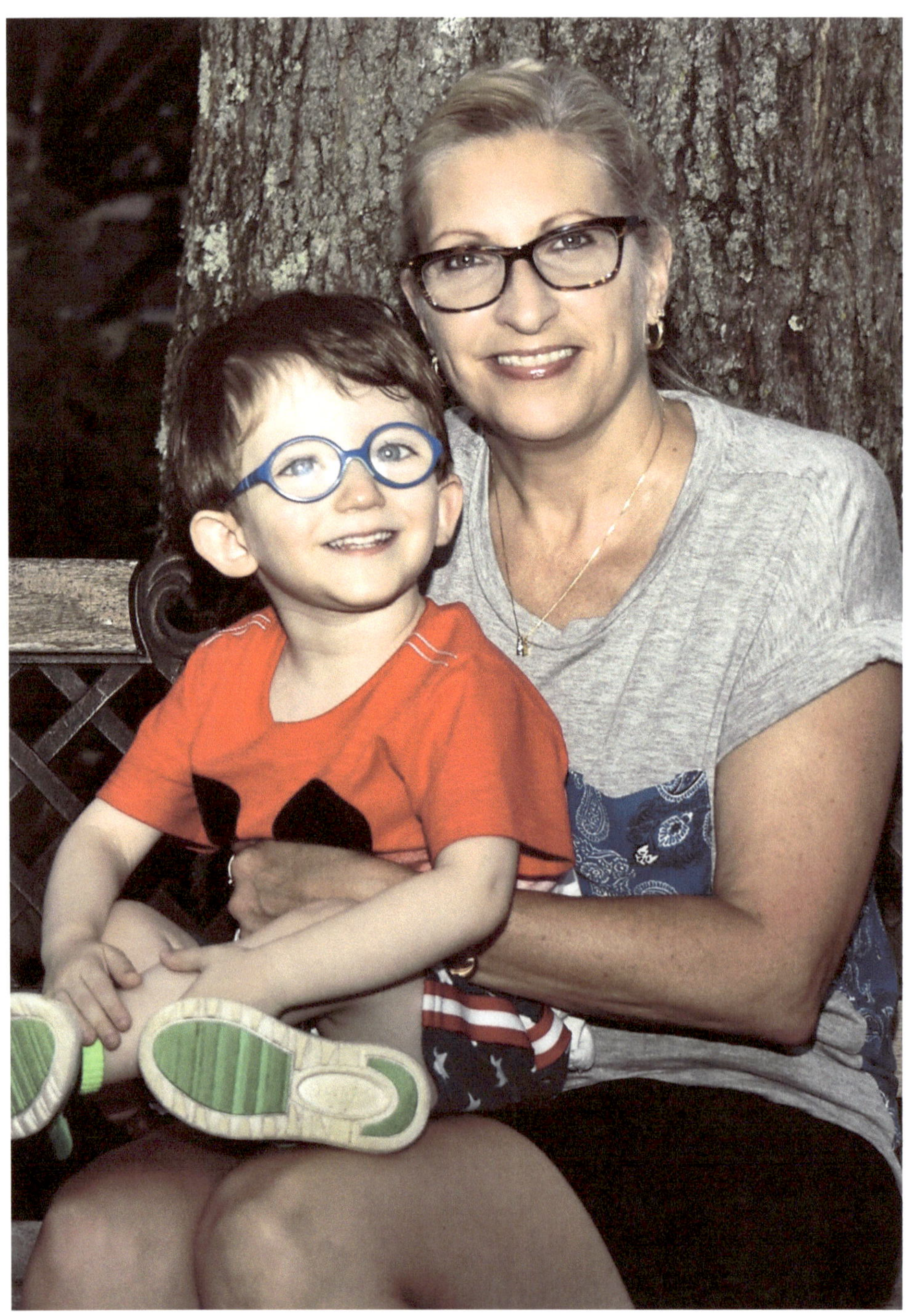

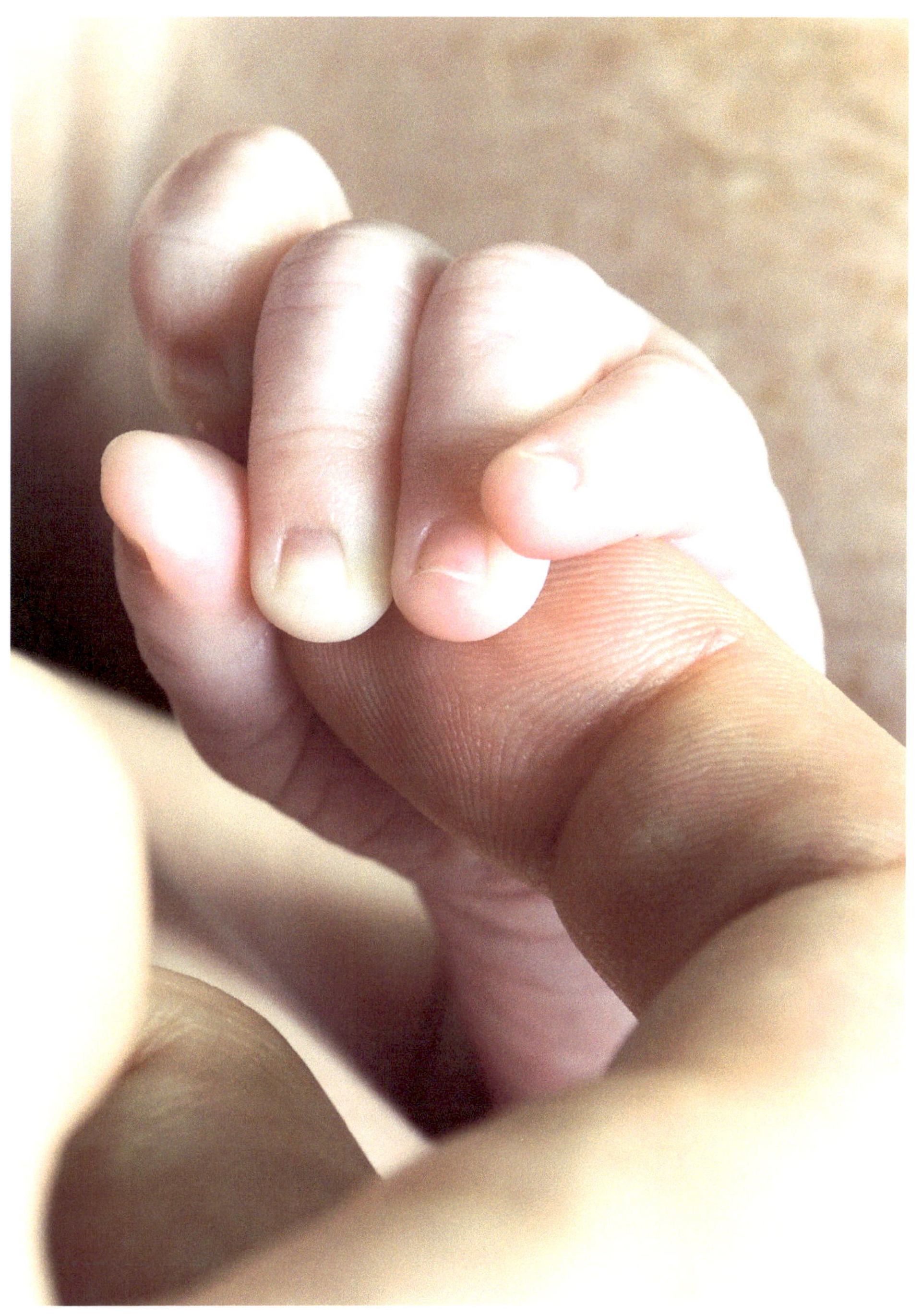

of all of life anew.

I'll share with you wisdom gained from

what I have been through.

I'll always be the other one

you know that you can trust.

Someday we'll part as I know we must,

but remember this as true from me

you know I would not lie. Love never

dies for someone you hold within your

heart no matter how much time goes by.

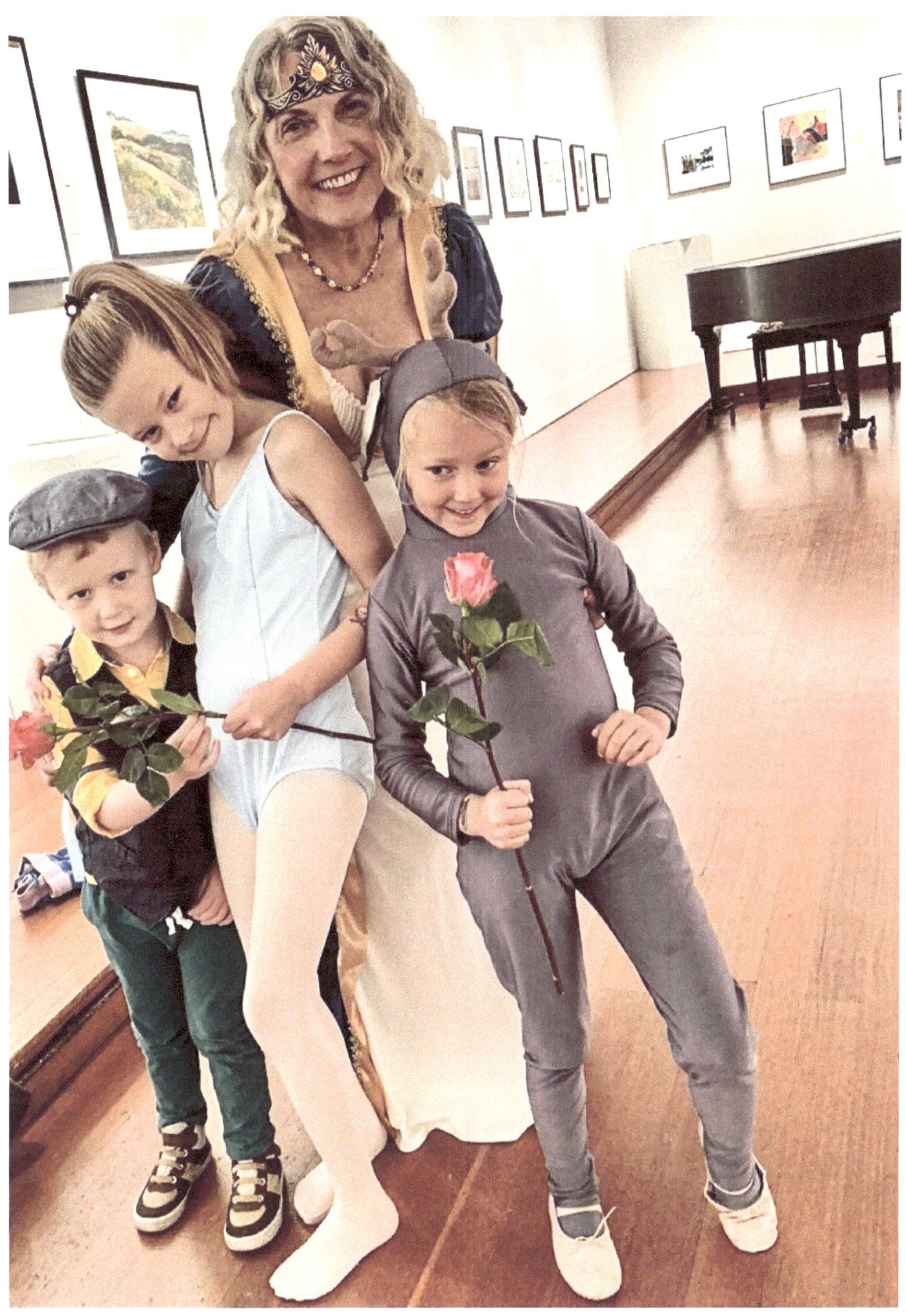

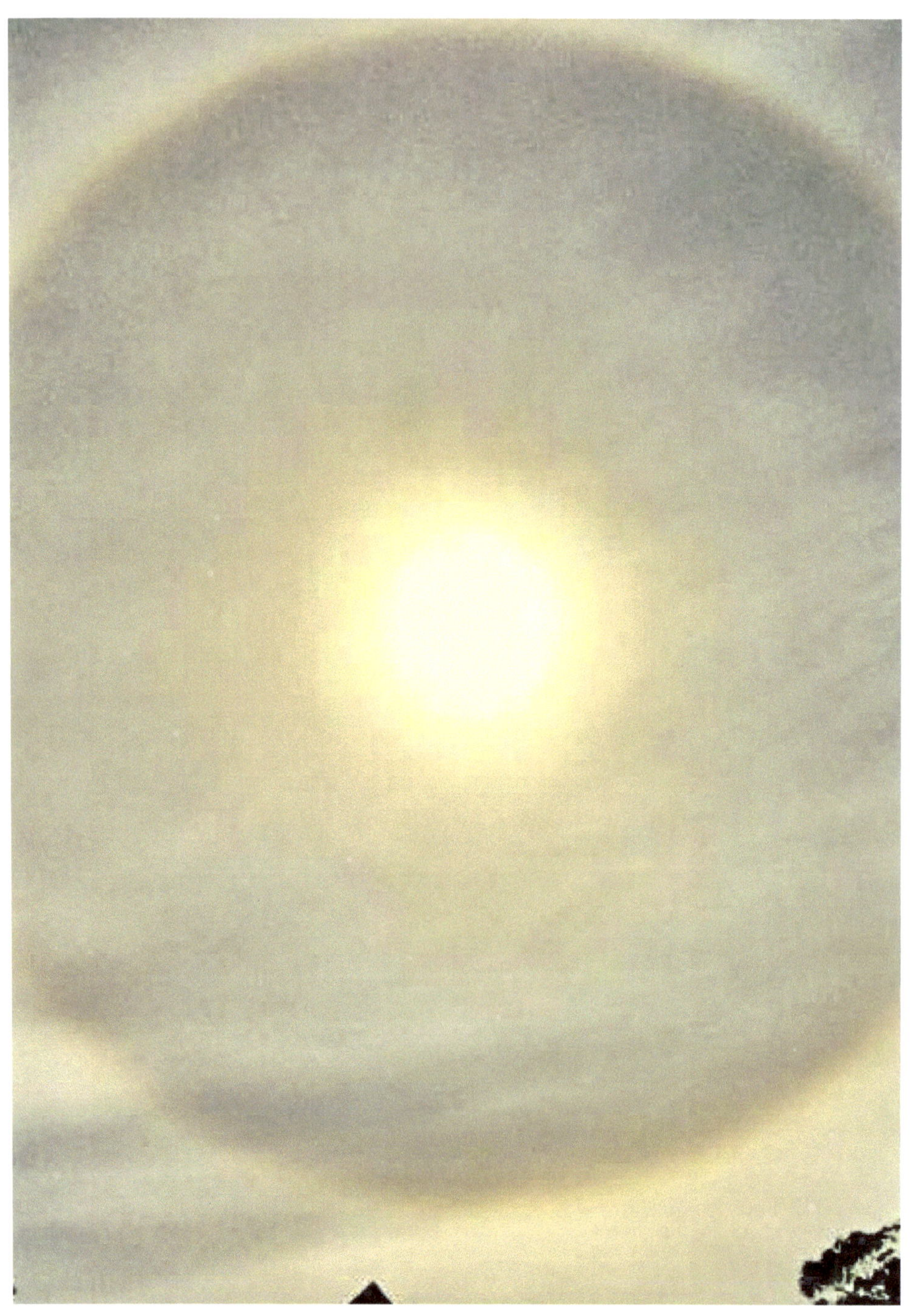

Pandemic

It is mid December

and I haven't had a hug since February.

My birthday came and went

without celebration,

without cake or a wish on candles,

without kisses from my grandchildren,

without warning of what had begun.

At the beginning, the very beginning.

Most of us had hoped

the news reports were wrong;

Most of us could not imagine how

our lives would soon resemble

those in a made for TV movie.

It was like preparing for a hurricane,

but no one boarded windows.

Hoarders emptied store shelves.

Toilet paper was in high demand.

There were no air raid sirens but

we were all at war.

The daily bombs that dropped

were the reports of rising death

counts and hospitals reaching capacity

around the world. The heroes of this war

are front line health care workers,

and volunteers testing new vaccines.

Shelter in place orders were put in place,

and conspiracy theorists seeded doubt.

I was an essential worker grateful

for the distraction. Grateful I was well

and not at home in solitude.

Still, everything went out of balance.

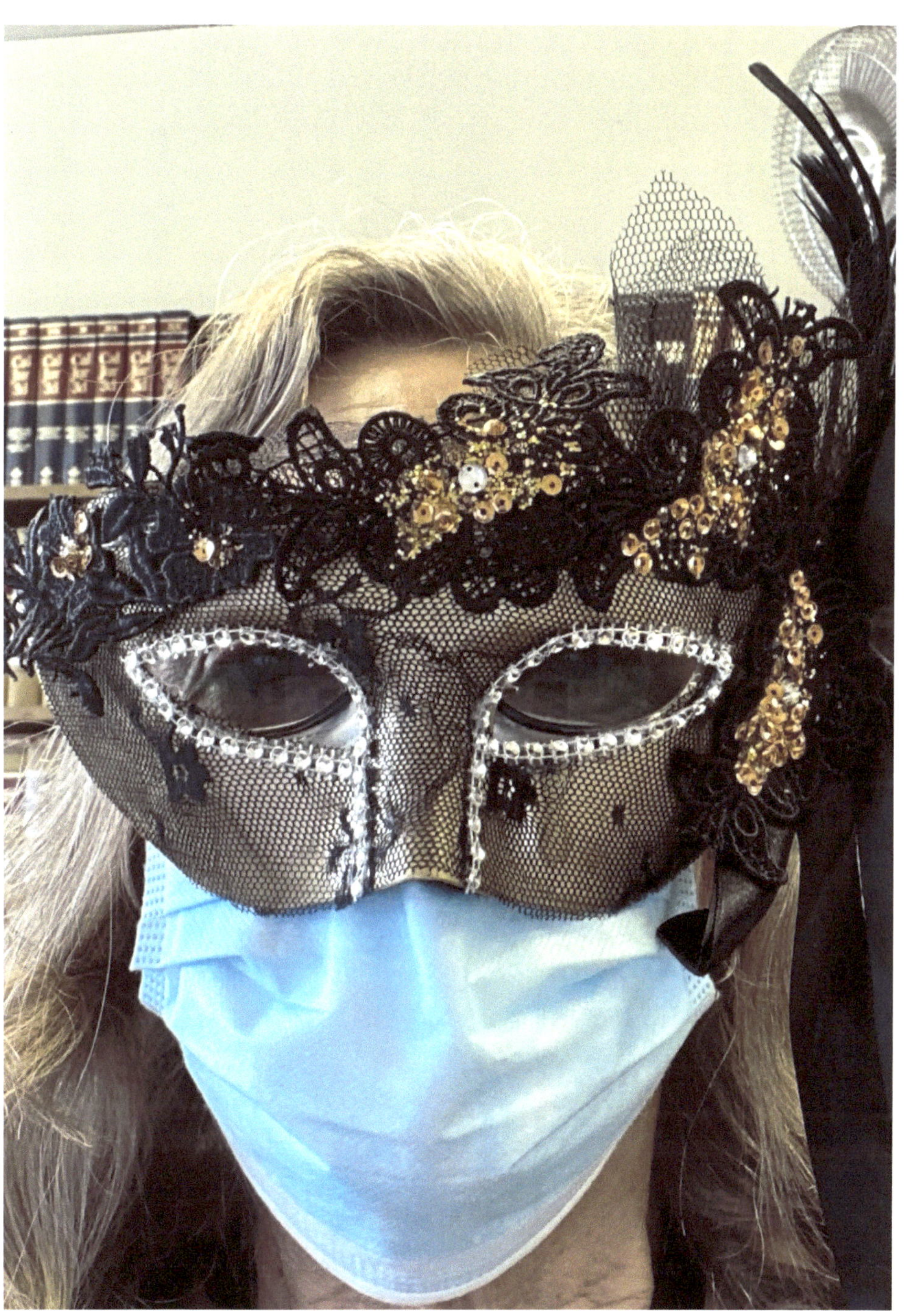

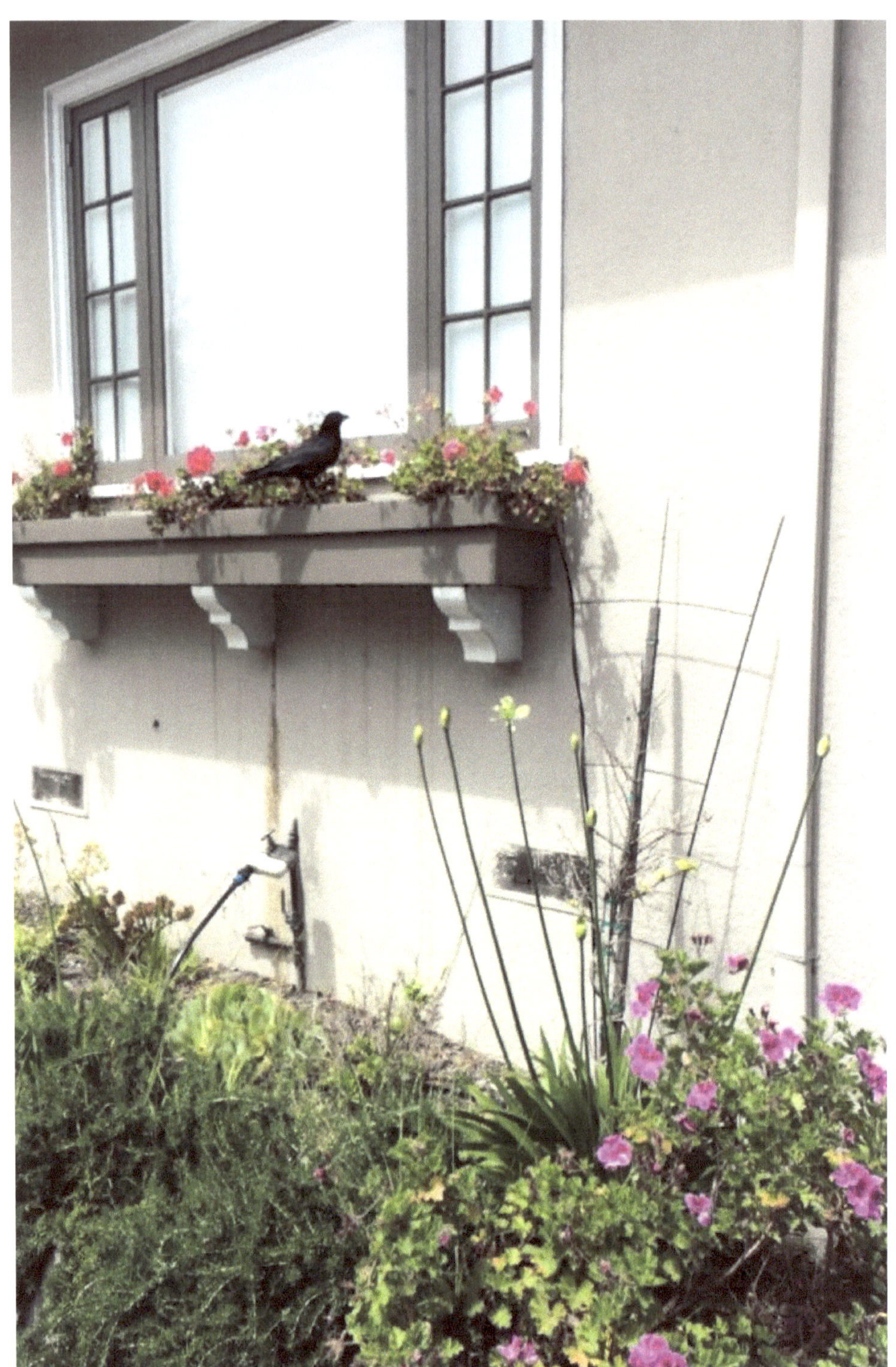

Guidelines were provided by the experts.
Wear a mask, do not touch your face,
wash your hands for twenty seconds, and
stay six feet away at all times from anyone
not in your household.
Everything once familiar is now lost
in the time before COVID-19.
I began to watch the daily numbers.
At first it was so shocking to learn
how many were quickly taken.
By July 20 2020 the world numbers
show the U.S. has the highest numbers-
3,961,429 cases and 143,834 deaths,
and the numbers, they keep rising.
Pandemic worst history-The Black Death-

estimated 75-200 million lives lost. The

number of COVID-19 cases

world wide total is 14,854,330

and the numbers, they keep rising.

Officially the virus was first introduced

in the U.S. in January, but there are

suspicions it was here amid

last winter's holiday season.

Everyone anxiously waits for news

of a vaccine and we monitor ourselves

carefully for symptoms, though most are

common to influenza.

No one is immune we learn

and parents keep their children close.

Patients communicate through

the doctors and nurses who hear their

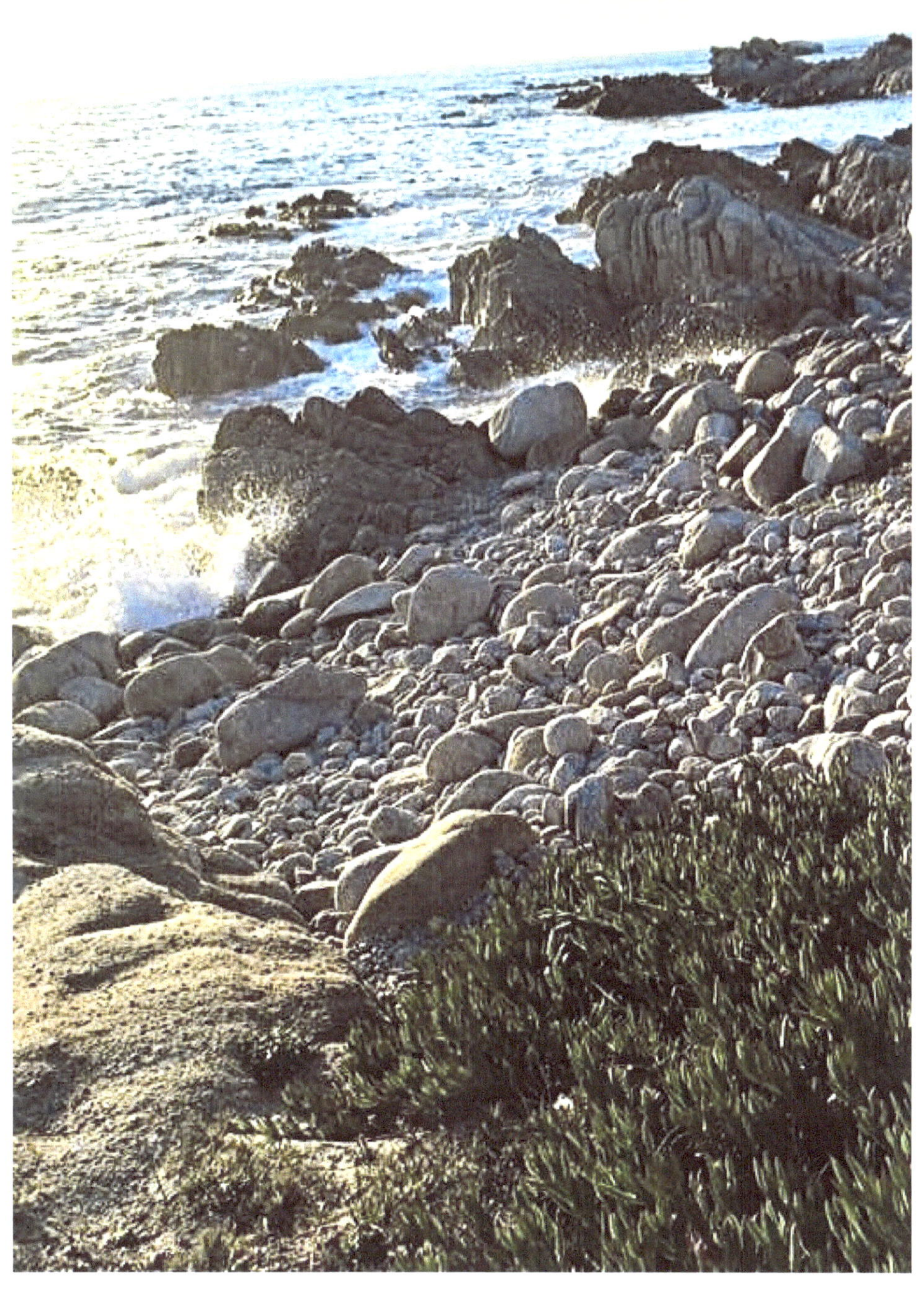

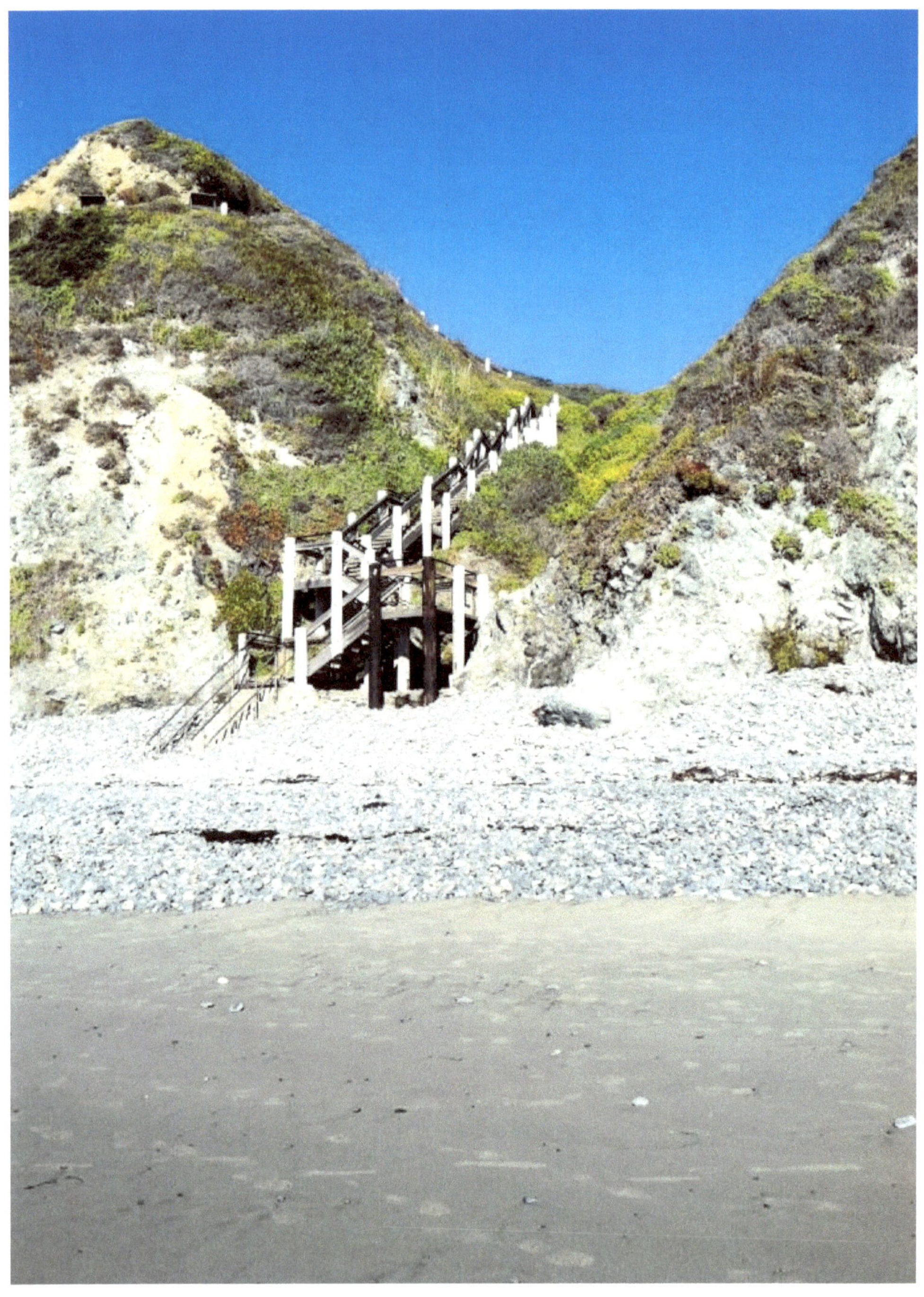

last parting words-it is heartbreaking.

August 1st-total deaths

U.S. reach 157,898; world, at 688,941

and the numbers, they keep rising.

September 26th-COVID-19

is still ravaging the world. Some European

countries are experiencing a second wave.

The U.S. braces for a hard winter

with 209,177 already dead

and the numbers, they keep rising.

October 25th-1,158,804 deaths worldwide

and the numbers keep rising.

November 12th-10,873,936 U.S. cases,

248,585 deaths

and the numbers keep rising.

January 24th-25,687,870 U.S. cases,

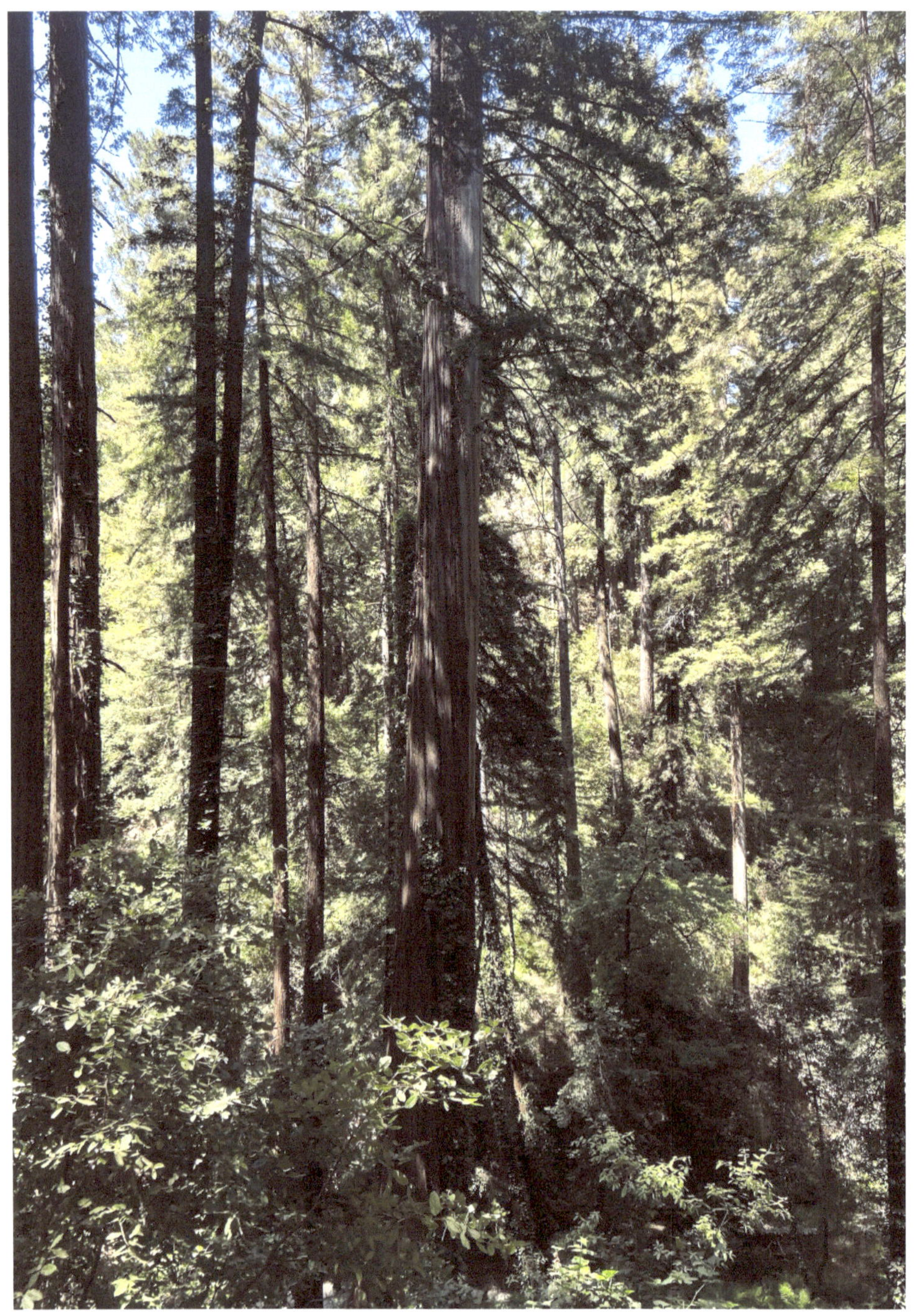

429,296 deaths

and the numbers keep rising.

February 21st total U.S. deaths 511,133;

total worldwide deaths 2,477,819

and the numbers they keep rising.

March 14th, 2021, now year two.

Vaccines are being distributed

and for the first time since this terrible

pandemic began most people

are feeling hopeful but do not dare

let down their guard.

There are some who for unknown reason

seem to have no regard for others

they selfishly put in peril.

The U.S. death toll has reached 547,234,

world deaths, 2,665,246 and the numbers,

they keep rising.
The curfews have been lifted,
though business not yet as usual.
Rebels test the mask mandate while
filming themselves like reality TV stars.
Seems a desperate way to the 15 minutes.
April 11th U.S. deaths 575,829,
case total 31,918,591;
world deaths 2,949,279,
world case total 136,630,352
and though slowing some, the numbers,
they keep rising.
The first vaccine of two brought relief,
like how one feels after averting disaster.
Nearly a year and half later
and we continue to live under a heightened anxiety.

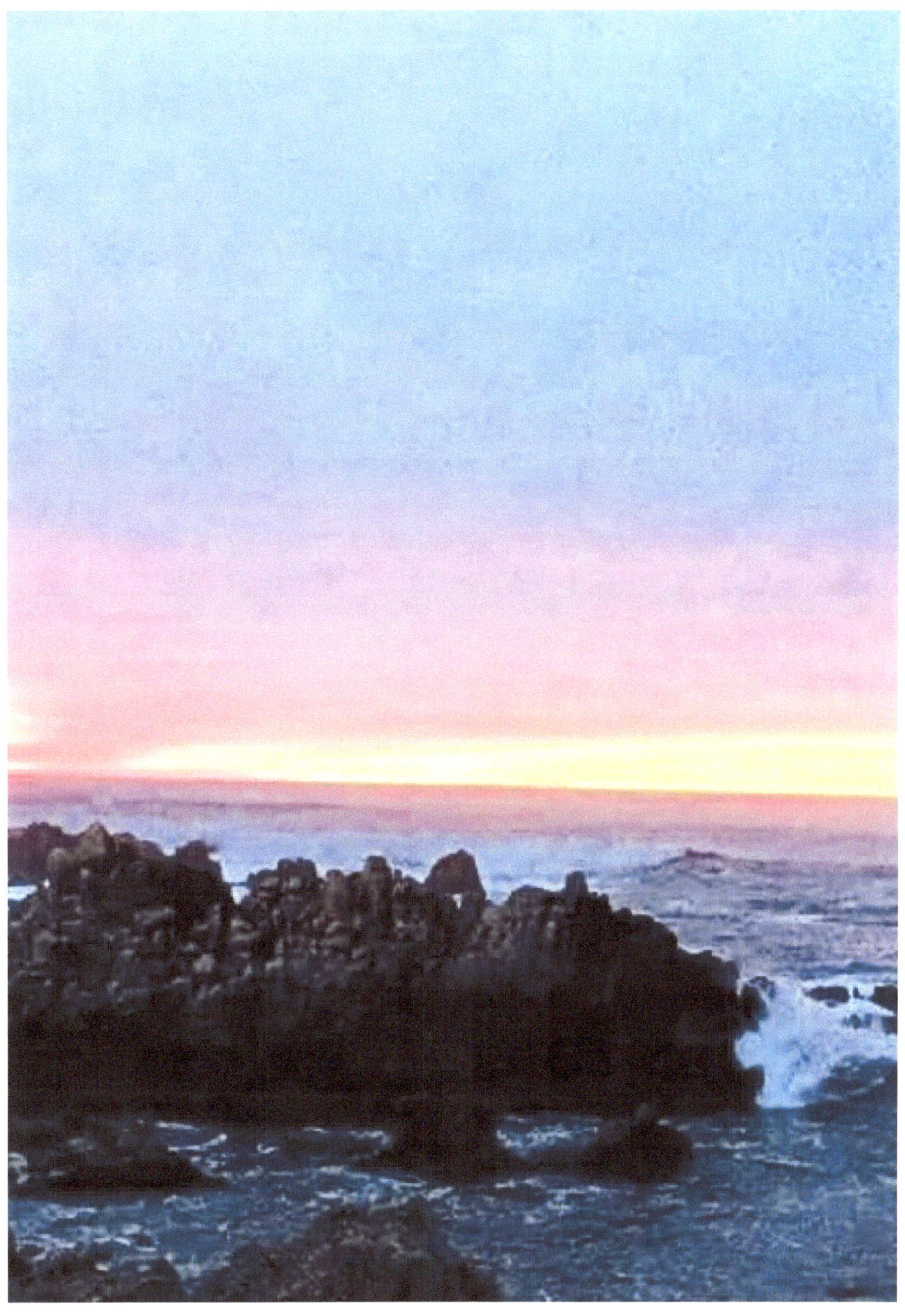

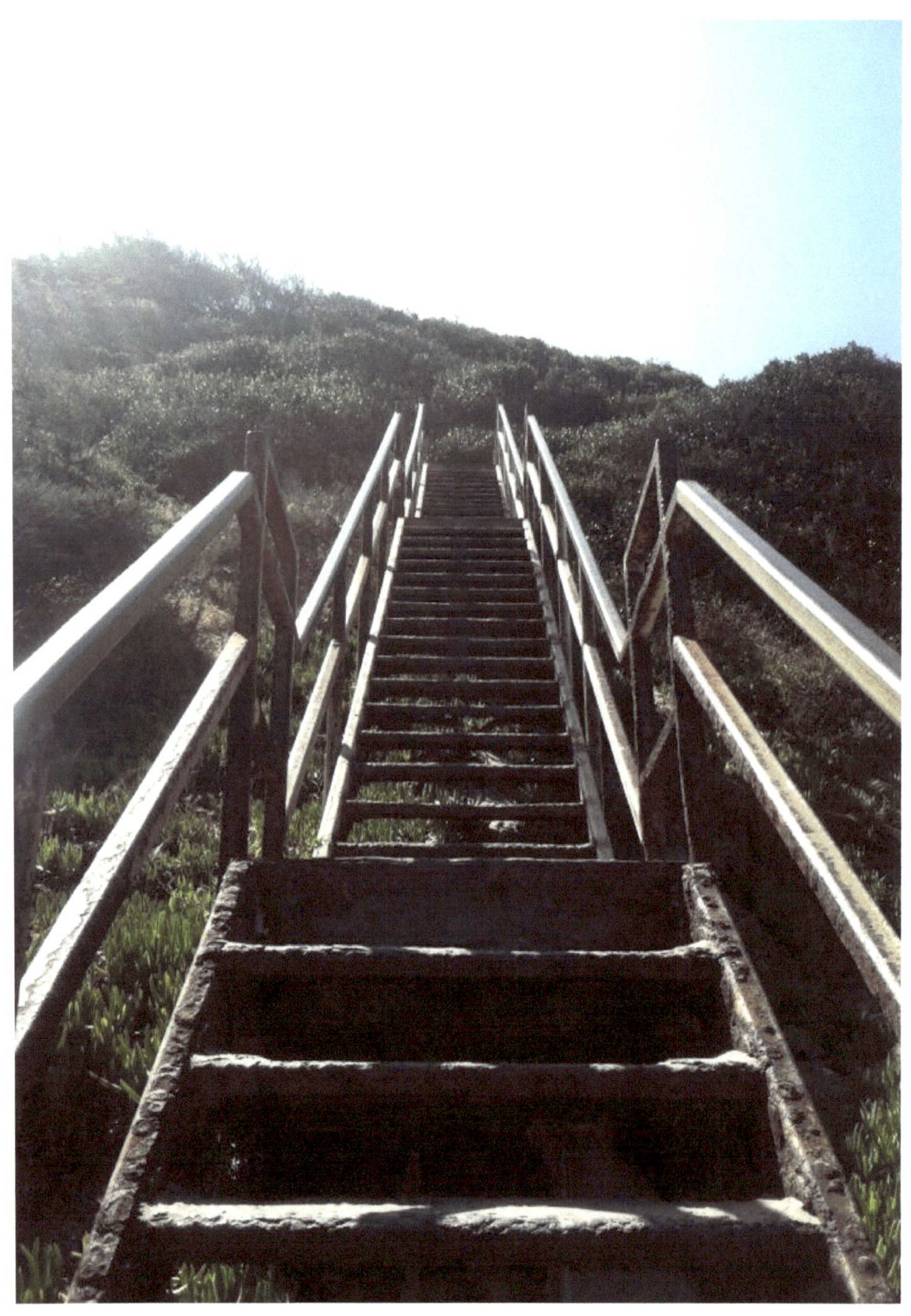

The stress is leaving it's mark on our furrowed brows.

No one knows how the virus may affect our future health.

With the second vaccine dose now done I feel safer; but, also

feel the rise of adrenaline each time I cough, have any chest pain,

or feel a headache coming on.

I still keep a watchful eye on the numbers.

It is May 29, 2021, Summer kick off.

There are 170,439,355 world cases,

3,543,985 deaths . . . and the numbers are still rising.

The Delta variant of the virus is spreading quickly

hitting hard the unvaccinated.

It is July 25, 2021 with 4,175,128 deaths

and 194,835,316 case infections documented worldwide

for this pandemic, not over as long as the numbers keep rising.

Grief

I heard the telephone but did not answer

because I did not want to know.

It was as if I could stop the world

from turning as long as

I did not hear the news.

I already knew because I saw you

driving down the street.

You were free and smiling

sitting next to your beloved son.

I knew you drove by to let me know

you were okay but my mind

refused to accept it. You see I had plans

to visit you during the Winter's holiday,

but my intentions could not keep you

from going home, it was your time.

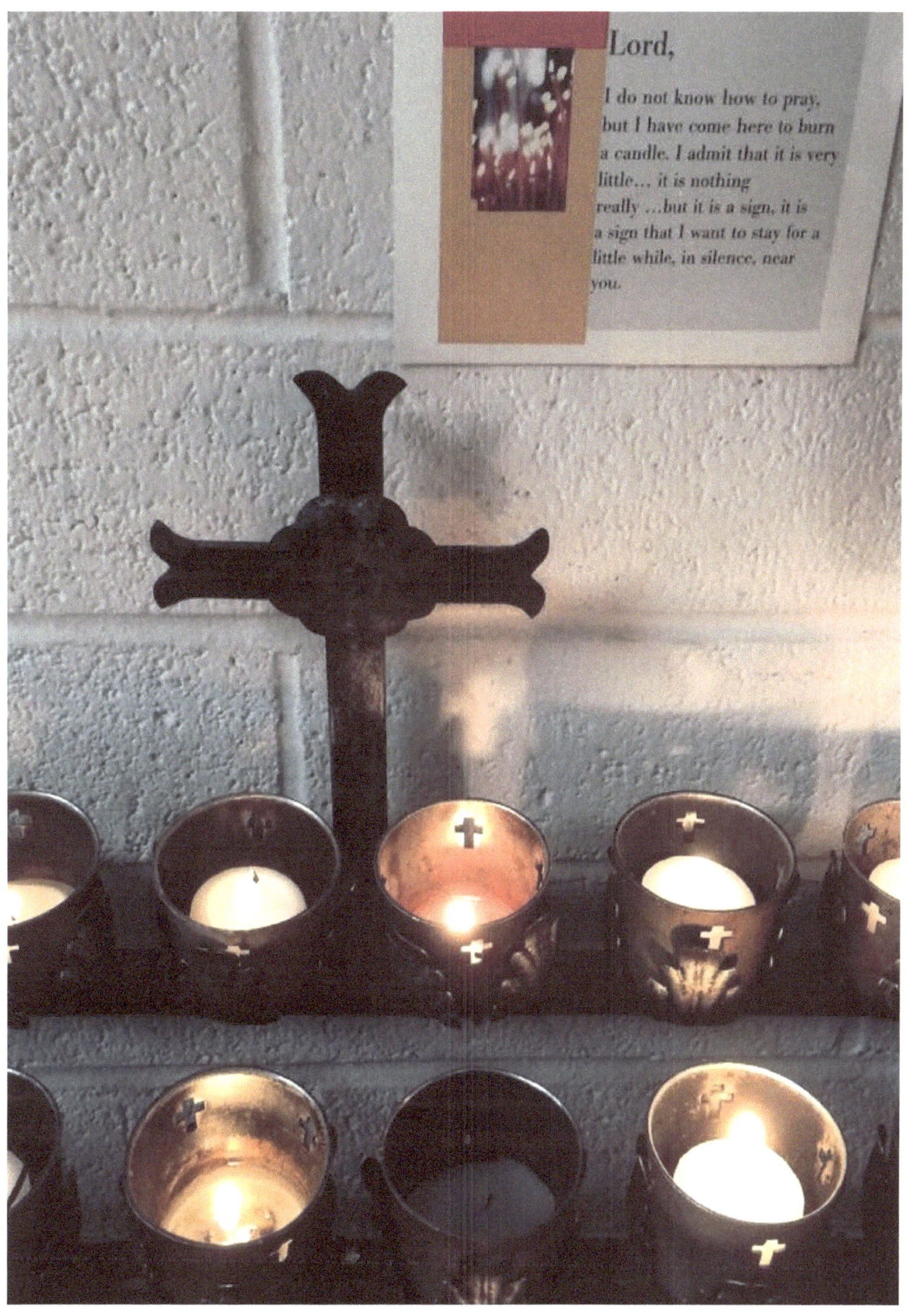
Lord,
I do not know how to pray,
but I have come here to burn
a candle. I admit that it is very
little… it is nothing
really …but it is a sign, it is
a sign that I want to stay for a
little while, in silence, near
you.

If I had known you were leaving
I would have walked with you awhile.
I would have held your hand.
I would have listened to your stories.
I would have tried to understand you.
I would have tried to make you laugh.
I would have sat with you in silence.
I would have told you that I loved you
if I had known it was goodbye.
You may not have known it then but your
influence embedded deeply in who I grew
to be. If I fail I try again and learn from
what went wrong. I stay calm, stand my
ground and buy it when on sale.

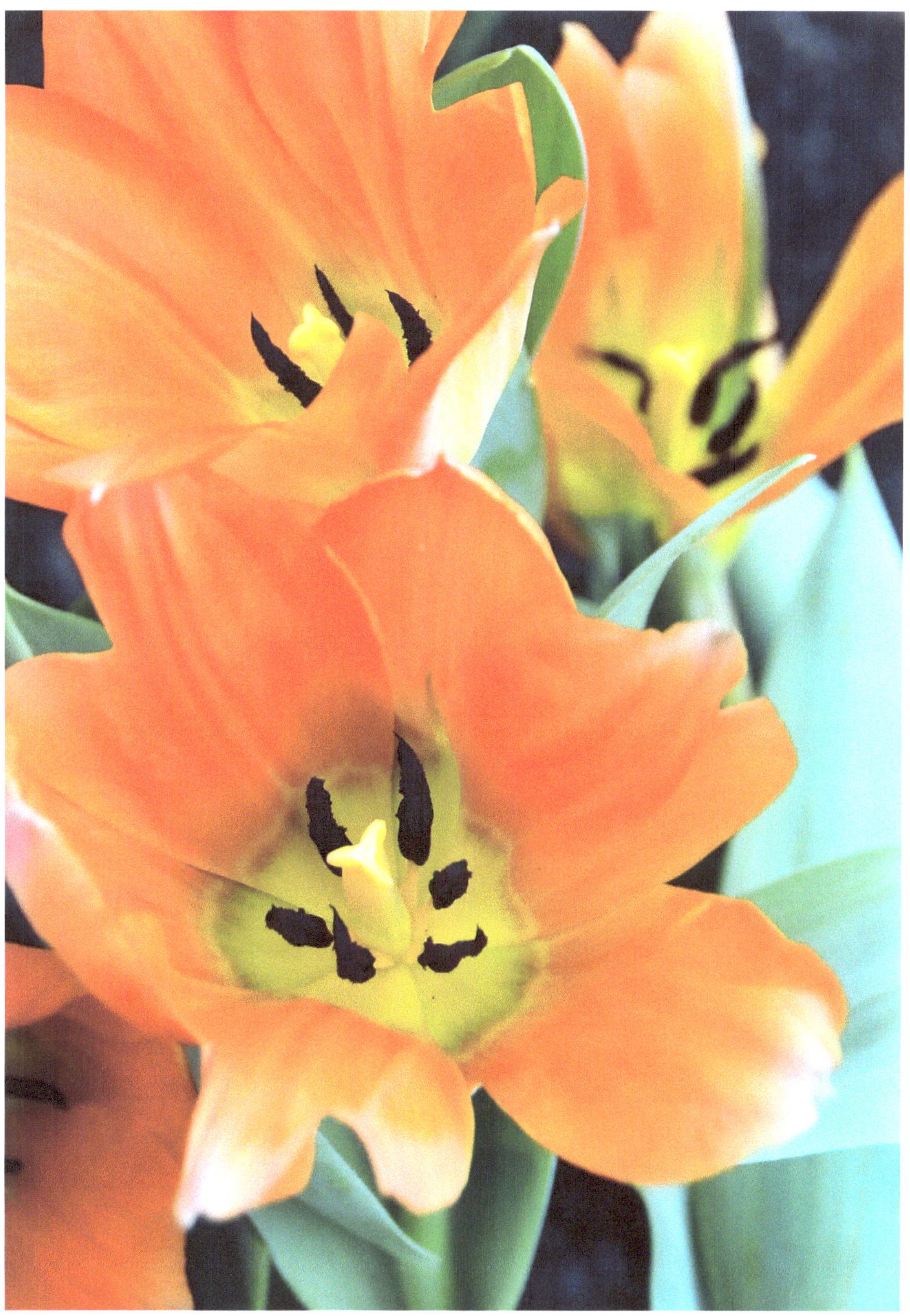

Worry

It is a Mother's unspoken job.

It comes naturally to all of us

no matter young or old.

No one has to teach us how,

we grasp it on our own.

With every move our children make

when they venture out of sight.

We worry until we see their face

or hear their voice alright.

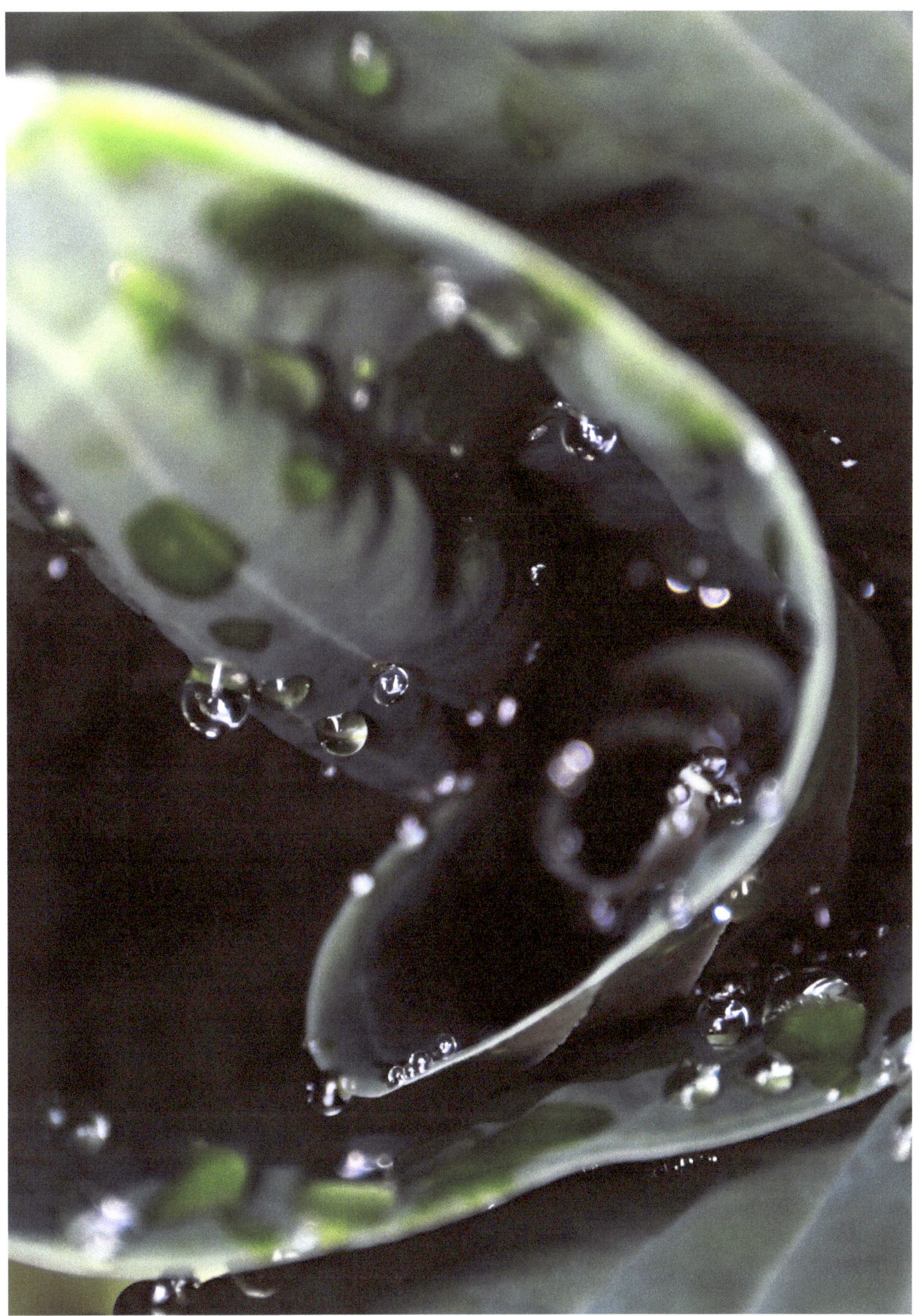

Acceptance

I'll never be a prima ballerina,

I'm more realistic now

Even all my secret dreams

Are fading into the backdrop

of the fabric making up my life.

I have come to terms with many things

that I know can never be

I'll never be a prima ballerina

I'll instead love the ballet.

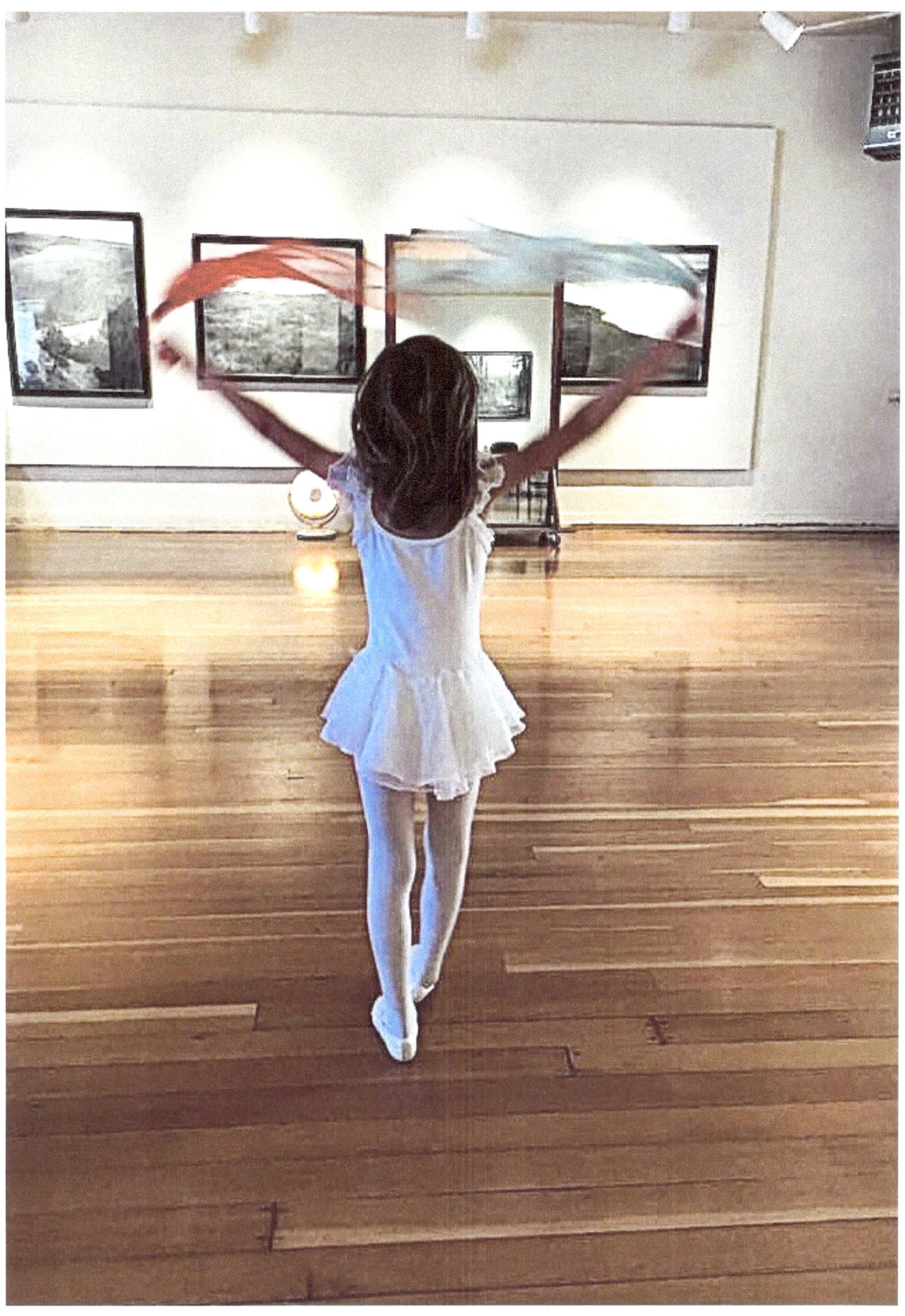

ABOUT THE AUTHOR

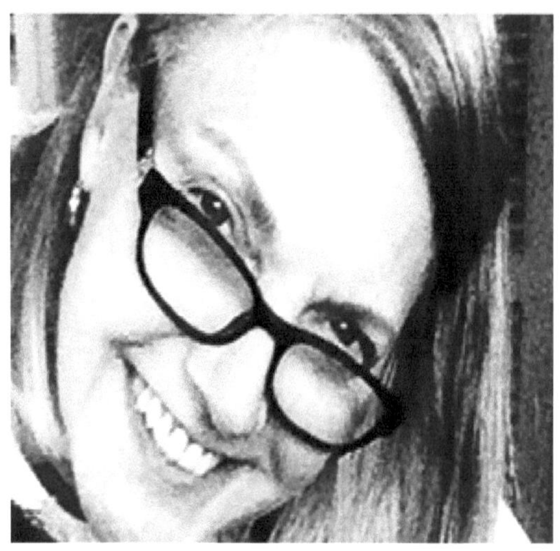

Carol writes on California's Central Coast

Carol 's other published titles:

- Jumping Jellybeans
- On Love, Poems from the Heart
- The Rolling Moon, a journey to understand alien abduction

ABOUT THE PHOTOGRAPHER

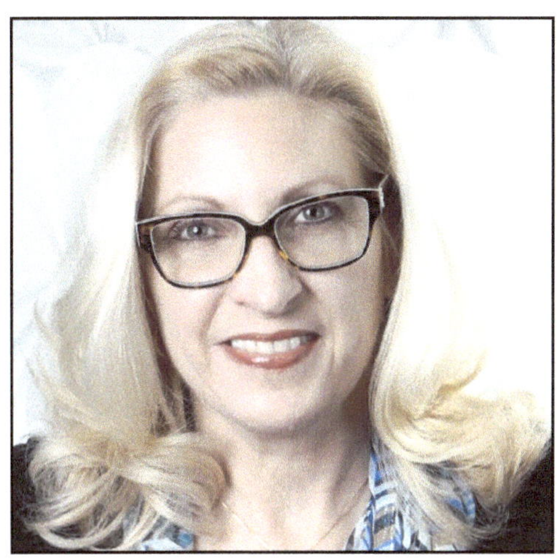

Diane is a Professional Photographer and Instructor in Western Pennsylvania.

Favorite quote from writer Forest Whitcraft: "One hundred years from now, it will not matter what my bank account was, how big my house was or what kind of a car I drove. But the world may be a little better because I was important in the life of a child."

www.ingramcontent.com/pod-product-compliance
Lightning Source LLC
LaVergne TN
LVHW052304100826
845147LV00006B/670

9780998348629